The Hampstead Clinic Psychoanalytic Library
(Concept Research Group)

VOLUME I

BASIC PSYCHOANALYTIC CONCEPTS ON THE LIBIDO THEORY

BASIC PSYCHOANALYTIC CONCEPTS ON THE LIBIDO THEORY

by

HUMBERTO NAGERA

and

S. BAKER, A. COLONNA, E. FIRST
A. GAVSHON, A. HOLDER, G. JONES
E. KOCH, M. LAUFER, D. MEERS,
L. NEURATH, K. REES

London

GEORGE ALLEN AND UNWIN LTD
RUSKIN HOUSE   MUSEUM STREET

PRINTED IN GREAT BRITAIN
in 11 on 12 pt Plantin
BY C. TINLING AND CO. LTD
LONDON AND PRESCOT

ACKNOWLEDGEMENTS AND COPYRIGHT NOTICES

Thanks are due to the members of the International Editorial Committee who undertook to read the drafts of the different concepts and made valuable suggestions. Among them: Dr D. Beres, Dr H. Hartmann, Dr H. Kohut, Dr M. Kris, Dr M. Schur, Dr A. F. Valenstein.

The editor and publishers also wish to thank a number of publishers for their kind permission to quote from the following material:

The Hogarth Press and the London Institute of Psychoanalysis for permission to quote from all volumes of the Standard Edition of the complete Psychological Works of Sigmund Freud.

W. W. Norton for permission to quote from the following publications of Freud:
Jokes and their Relation to the Unconscious
The Claims of Psychoanalysis to Scientific Interest
An Outline of Psychoanalysis
New Introductory Lectures on Psycho-analysis
Totem and Taboo
Leonardo da Vinci
An Autobiographical Study
The Question of Lay Analysis
Civilization and its Discontents
The Ego and the Id.

Liveright for permission to quote from the following publications of Freud:
Five Lectures on Psychoanalysis
Group Psychology and the Analysis of the Ego
Beyond the Pleasure Principle
Introductory Lectures on Psychoanalysis.

ACKNOWLEDGEMENTS AND COPYRIGHT NOTICES

Routledge for permission to quote from the following publications of Freud:
Jokes and their Relation to the Unconscious
The Claims of Psychoanalysis to Scientific Interest
Totem and Taboo
Leonardo da Vinci

FOREWORD TO
THE HAMPSTEAD CLINIC LIBRARY

The series of publications of which the present volume forms a part, will be welcomed by all those readers who are concerned with the history of psychoanalytic concepts and interested to follow the vicissitudes of their fate through the theoretical, clinical and technical writings of psychoanalytic authors. On the one hand, these fates may strike us as being very different from each other. On the other hand, it proves not too difficult to single out some common trends and to explore the reasons for them.

There are some terms and concepts which served an important function for psychoanalysis in its earliest years because of their being simple and all-embracing such as for example the notion of a *'complex'*. Even the lay public understood more or less easily that what was meant thereby was any cluster of impulses, emotions, thoughts, etc. which have their roots in the unconscious and, exerting their influence from there, give rise to anxiety, defences and symptom formation in the conscious mind. Accordingly, the term was used widely as a form of psychological short-hand. 'Father-Complex', 'Mother-Complex', 'Guilt-Complex', 'Inferiority-Complex', etc. became familiar notions. Nevertheless, in due course, added psychoanalytical findings about the child's relationship to his parents, about the early mother-infant tie and its consequences, about the complexities of lacking self-esteem and feelings of insufficiency and inferiority demanded more precise conceptualization. The very omnibus nature of the term could not but lead to its, at least partial, abandonment. All that remained from it were the terms 'Oedipus-Complex' to designate the experiences centred around the triangular relationships of the phallic phase, and 'Castration-Complex' for the anxieties, repressed wishes, etc. concerning the loss or lack of the male sexual organ.

If, in the former instance, a general concept was split up to make room for more specific meanings, in other instances concepts took turns in the opposite direction. After starting out as concrete, well-defined descriptions of circumscribed psychic events, they were applied by many authors to an ever-widening circle of phenomena until their connotation became increasingly vague and imprecise and until finally special efforts had to be made to re-define them,

9

to restrict their sphere of application and to invest them once more with precision and significance. This is what happened, for example, to the concepts of '*Transference*' and of '*Trauma*'.

The concept and term 'transference' was designed originally to establish the fact that the realistic relationship between analyst and patient is invariably distorted by phantasies and object-relations which stem from the patient's past and that these very distortions can be turned into a technical tool to reveal the patient's past pathogenic history. In present days, the meaning of the term has been widened to the extent that it comprises whatever happens between analyst and patient regardless of its derivation and of the reasons for its happening.

A 'trauma' or 'traumatic happening' meant originally an (external or internal) event of a magnitude with which the individual's ego is unable to deal, i.e. a sudden influx of excitation, massive enough to break through the ego's normal stimulus barrier. To this purely quantitative meaning of the term were added in time all sorts of qualifications (such as cumulative, retrospective, silent, beneficial), until the concept ended up as more or less synonymous with the notion of a pathogenic event in general.

Psychoanalytic concepts may be overtaken also by a further fate, which is perhaps of even greater significance. Most of them owe their origin to a particular era of psychoanalytic theory, or to a particular field of clinical application, or to a particular mode of technique. Since any of the backgrounds in which they are rooted, are open to change, this should lead either to a corresponding change in the concepts or to their abandonment. But, most frequently, this has failed to happen. Many concepts are carried forward through the changing scene of psychoanalytic theory and practice without sufficient thought being given to their necessary alteration or re-definition.

A case in kind is the concept of '*acting out*'. It was created at the very outset of technical thinking and teaching, tied to the treatment of neurotic patients, and it characterized originally a specific reaction of these patients to the psychoanalytic technique, namely that certain items of their past, when retrieved from the unconscious, did not return to conscious memory but revealed themselves instead in behaviour, were 'acted on', or 'acted out' instead of being remembered. By now, this clear distinction between remembering the recovered past and re-living it has been obscured; the term 'acting out' is used out of this context, notably for patients such as adolescents, delinquents or psychotics whose impulse-ridden behaviour is part of their original pathology and not the direct consequence of analytic work done on the ego's defences against the repressed unconscious.

It was in this state of affairs that *Dr H. Nagera* initiated his enquiry into the history of psychoanalytic thinking. Assisted by a team of analytic workers, trained in the Hampstead Child-Therapy Course and Clinic, he set out to trace the course of basic psycho-analytic concepts from their first appearance through their changes in the twenty-three volumes of the Standard Edition of the Complete Psychological Works of Sigmund Freud, i.e. to a point from where they are meant to be taken further to include the writings of the most important authors of the post-Freudian era.

Dr Nagera's aim in this venture was a fourfold one:

to facilitate for readers of psychoanalytic literature the under-standing of psychoanalytic thought and of the terminology in which it is expressed;

to understand and define concepts, not only according to their individual significance, but also according to their relevance for the particular historical phase of psychoanalytic theory within which they have arisen;

to induce psychoanalytic authors to use their terms and con-cepts more precisely with regard for the theoretical framework to which they owe their origin, and to reduce thereby the many sources of misunderstanding and confusion which govern the psychoanalytic literature at present;

finally, to create for students of psychoanalysis the opportunity to embark on a course of independent reading and study, linked to a scholarly aim and designed to promote their critical and constructive thinking on matters of theory-formation.

Anna Freud, London, August 1968

CONTENTS

CONTENTS

INTRODUCTION

This volume is a sample of scholastic research work carried out at the Hampstead Child-Therapy Course and Clinic relating to the study of a large number of pre-selected basic psychoanalytic concepts postulated and developed by Freud in his psychoanalytic writings, spanning the time from his earliest to his latest conceptualizations.

This research work has been carried out during the last six years by the Concept Research Group. These drafts on basic concepts are in no way meant to replace the study of Freud's works themselves. On the contrary, they are intended as a guide to help the student in that very aim.

The group's method has been to assign to each of its members one pre-selected concept at a time. This member's task then is to extract all the relevant material from Freud's published papers, books, correspondence, Minutes of the Meetings of the Vienna Psychoanalytic Society, etc., and to prepare a written summary of a given concept for discussion. This first draft is referred to as the 'personal draft' and is circulated among members some time before it is due for discussion.

As far as possible the draft makes use of 'literal quotations', giving at the same time the source of the quotations. This facilitates the study of the drafts by the group members who meet weekly to discuss the personal drafts. On the basis of the general discussion by the Group a second draft is produced which we designate as the 'group draft'.

Our aims are multiple and are very much in accordance with the views expressed by Hartmann, Kris and Loewenstein in their paper 'The Function of Theory in Psychoanalysis'[1] and in other publications.

Like these authors, we believe that Freud's views are often misrepresented in a considerable number of the vast amount of psychoanalytic writings due to the fact that certain of Freud's

[1] Hartmann, H., Kris, E., Loewenstein, R. M., 'The Function of Theory in Psychoanalysis', *Drives, Affects and Behaviour*, International Universities Press, Inc., New York, 1953.

statements are not always evaluated within their proper context. Thus, not infrequently, specific aspects are torn out of a long historical line of theoretical development and isolated from the rest, and similarly one or the other phase of psychoanalytic thinking is given undue emphasis out of context. Such misrepresentations are apt to convey the erroneous impression that whatever aspect has been singled out embraces all that Freud or psychoanalysis had ever to say on some specific topic. In this sense we very much endorse the statement made by Hartmann, Kris and Loewenstein that 'quoting Freud is, as a rule, meaningful only if it is part of a laborious but unavoidable attempt to gain insight into the position of the quoted passage within the development of Freud's thought'.[1] This is precisely one of the major aims of the Concept Research Group.

We were similarly prompted for what we felt with Hartmann, Kris and Loewenstein, to be 'the disregard for the psychoanalytic theory as a coherent set of assumptions'.[2] 'Freud's hypotheses are interrelated in a systematic way: there is a hierarchy of hypothesis in their relevance, their closeness to observation, their degree of verification. It is none the less true that there exists no comprehensive presentation of analysis from this angle. Here again recourse to the historical approach seems imperative . . . by showing the actual problems in their right proportions and in their right perspective.'[3]

Another important factor is the realization that Freud made many statements in the course of developing his theories which he withdrew or modified in subsequent works. This in itself constitutes a major source of frequent misrepresentation of Freud's views. One of the aims of this work, in which we try to evaluate Freud's basic psychoanalytic concepts in their historical context, is precisely to avoid such pitfalls and misrepresentations.

We further agree with Hartmann, Kris and Loewenstein that a serious danger of misrepresentation exists when there is an in-

[1] Hartmann, H., 'The Development of the Ego Concept in Freud's Work', I.J.P., Vol. XXXVII, Part VI, 1956. (Paper read at the Freud Centenary Meeting of the British Psycho-Analytical Society, May 5, 1956.)
[2] Hartmann, H., Kris, E., Loewenstein, R. M., 'The Function of Theory in Psychoanalysis', Drives, Affects and Behaviour, International Universities Press, Inc., New York, 1953, p. 23.
[3] Hartmann, H., 'The Development of the Ego Concept in Freud's Work', I.J.P., Vol. XXXVII, Part VI, London 1956, p. 425.

sufficient understanding of the hierarchy of psychoanalytic propositions. It is therefore essential to have a clear understanding of how the different parts of psychoanalytic theoretical propositions fit together, both when quoting and when attempting new formulations.

We are planning to publish the remainder of the work of the Concept Research Group up to the present moment in the near future in order to make it available to teachers and students in the psychoanalytic and related fields. We think that this contribution will be of special value and interest to any student of Freud, especially students in training who will have an encyclopaedic review of basic psychoanalytic concepts in an extremely condensed but meaningful way. From these summaries of concepts the student can readily find his way back to Freud's work in order to pursue and become more fully acquainted with his formulations. In this way he can study specific aspects in the development of the theory while being able, at the same time, to get a more comprehensive and over-all view of the particular topic and its relations with other aspects of the theory. We believe that our work will be similarly useful to lecturers and seminar leaders, to research workers in the field of psychoanalysis and related fields and to those writing papers which require a review of Freud's statements with regard to a specific topic. Altogether this form of scholastic research may help to avoid confusion, constant reformulations and the introduction of new terms when authors in fact refer to 'concepts' already clearly described by Freud in the past. This work may well help to open the way to standardize and find some measure of agreement as to the precise meaning of terms used in psychoanalysis today.

Although we have taken as much care as possible to be comprehensive and to avoid misrepresentations, experience has taught us that we can have no claim to perfection or completeness. It is practically impossible, within a vast and complex volume of theory such as Freud's life output represents, not to overlook or even slightly to misrepresent one or another aspect or set of factors. Furthermore, the capacity to comprehend and the level of insight possible for any given person or group of persons engaged in such work increases as the work proceeds. Thus certain formulations become more meaningful, are suddenly understood in a new light, assume a different significance, etc. Because of our realization of potential shortcomings we hope that future readers of these con-

B

cepts will contribute to complete and clarify the work which the Concept Group has started, by drawing our attention to relevant material which has been either overlooked, misrepresented or not understood in its full significance.

It is hoped that in this way the Concepts will become more and more representative and complete in the course of time.

DR HUMBERTO NAGERA.

SOURCE, PRESSURE, AIM AND OBJECT OF THE SEXUAL COMPONENT INSTINCT

SEE ALSO: *especially Erotogenic Zones, Component Instincts, Instincts, Aggression, Instinct and Drive, Cathexis.*

Freud first described the sexual instinct's source, aim and object in his *Three Essays on Sexuality*, 1905, and amplified this, in the light of his developing theories, in later footnotes to the *Three Essays*, and also in 'Instincts and their Vicissitudes', 1915, and in the *New Introductory Lectures*, 1933.

'We can distinguish an instinct's source, object and aim. Its source is a state of excitation in the body, its aim is the removal of that excitation; on its path from its source to its aim the instinct becomes operative psychically.'[1]

In 1915 he defined instinct as 'a concept on the frontier between the mental and the somatic, as the psychical representative of the stimuli originating from within the organism and reaching the mind, as a measure of the demand made upon the mind for work in consequence of its connection with the body'.[2]

The source
The source of an instinct is a process of excitation occurring in an organ. Excitations of two kinds arise from the somatic organs, based upon differences of a chemical nature. One of these we describe as being specifically sexual, and the organ concerned as the 'erotogenic zone' of the sexual component instinct arising from it.[3] An erotogenic zone is a part of the skin or mucous membrane in which stimuli of a certain sort evoke a feeling of pleasure possessing a particular quality. 'The character of erotogenicity can be attached to some parts of the body in a particularly marked way ... [though] any other part of the skin or mucous membrane

---

[1] (1933a) *New Introductory Lectures on Psycho-Analysis*, the Standard Edition of the Complete Psychological Works of Sigmund Freud (hereafter referred to as S.E.), Vol. 22, p. 96.
[2] (1915c) 'Instincts and their Vicissitudes', S.E., Vol. 14, p. 121 f.
[3] (1905d) *Three Essays on the Theory of Sexuality*, S.E., Vol. 7, p. 168.

19

can take over the functions of an erotogenic zone . . .' The 'satis-faction must have been previously experienced in order to have left behind a need for its repetition'. The need for repetition of the satisfaction reveals itself in 'a peculiar feeling of tension, possessing rather, the character of unpleasure, and by a sensation of itching or stimulation which is centrally conditioned and projected on to the peripheral erotogenic zone'.[1] Sexual excitation arises in several ways, i.e. (a) as a reproduction of a satisfaction experienced in connection with other organic processes—e.g. feeding, defeca-ting, urination; (b) through appropriate peripheral stimulation of erotogenic zones and (c) as the result of various kinds of stimula-tion which can arouse erotogenic effects in the skin—mechanical agitation of the body, muscular activities and also intense affective processes and intellectual work.[2] '. . . there are present in the organism contrivances which bring it about that in the case of a great number of internal processes sexual excitation arises as a concomitant effect, as soon as the intensity of those processes passes beyond certain quantitative limits. What we have called the component instincts of sexuality are either derived directly from these internal sources or are composed of elements both from those sources and from the erotogenic zones.' Individual sexual constitutions will vary according to the varying development of the erotogenic zones and of the internal sources.[3]

Freud describes how the main erotogenic zones, the oral, anal, phallic are successively stimulated because of the organic functions with which they are associated. He also says that the order in which the various instinctual impulses come into activity seems to be phylogenetically determined, so too does the length of time during which they are able to manifest themselves before they succumb to the effects of some freshly emerging instinctual impulse, or to some typical repression.[4]

Freud also stated that '. . . it may be supposed that, as a result of an appropriate stimulation of the erotogenic zones, or in other circumstances that are accompanied by an onset of sexual excita-tion, some substance that is disseminated generally throughout the organism becomes decomposed and the products of its decomposi-

---

[1] ibid., p. 183 f.
[2] ibid., pp. 200–4.   [3] ibid., p. 204 f.
[4] (1933a) *New Introductory Lectures on Psycho-Analysis*, S.E., Vol. 22, p. 93 f., cf. also (1905d) *Three Essays on the Theory of Sexuality*, S.E., Vol. 7, p. 241.

tion give rise to a specific stimulus which acts on the reproductive organs or upon a spinal centre related to them'.[1] (Strachey comments that it is worth noting how small a modification was made necessary in Freud's hypothesis by the discovery of sex hormones.)

The pressure

In 'Instincts and their Vicissitudes' Freud also defines what he means by the pressure of an instinct—namely ' . . . the amount of force or the measure of the demand for work which it represents. The characteristic of exercising pressure is common to all instincts; it is in fact their very essence'.[2] An instinct 'operates as a constant force, and (is such) that the subject cannot avoid it by flight, as is possible with an external stimulus'. Every instinct is a piece of activity.[3]

The aim

Freud stated that though people 'speak of "active" and "passive" instincts', it 'would be more correct to speak of instincts with active and passive aims: for an expenditure of activity is needed to achieve a passive aim as well'. He continued: 'The aim can be achieved in the subject's own body: as a rule an internal object is brought in, in regard to which the instinct achieves its external aim; its internal aim invariably remains the bodily change which is felt as satisfaction'.[4] In 'Instincts and their Viccissitudes' he again explained that the 'aim of an instinct is in every instance satisfaction, which can only be obtained by removing the state of stimulation at the source of the instinct. But although the ultimate aim of each instinct remain unchangeable, there may yet be different paths leading to the same ultimate aim; so that an instinct may be found to have various nearer or intermediate aims, which are combined or interchanged with one another'.[5]

The sexual aim of the infant is 'dominated by an erotogenic zone'.[6] It 'consists in obtaining satisfaction by means of an appropriate stimulation of the erotogenic zone . . . replacing the projected sensation of stimulation in the erotogenic zone by an

[1] (1950d) *Three Essays on the Theory of Sexuality*, S.E., Vol. 7, p. 216 n.
[2] (1915e) 'The Unconscious', S.E., Vol. 14, p. 122.
[3] (1933a) *New Introductory Lectures on Psycho-Analysis*, S.E., Vol. 22, p. 96.
[4] ibid., p. 96.
[5] (1915c) 'Instincts and their Vicissitudes', S.E., Vol. 14, p. 122.
[6] (1905d) *Three Essays on the Theory of Sexuality*, S.E., Vol. 7, p. 182.

external stimulus which removes that sensation by producing a feeling of satisfaction'.[1]

The normal sexual aim in adults 'is regarded as being the union of the genitals in the act known as copulation, which leads to a release of the sexual tension and a temporary extinction of the sexual instinct'.[2] Freud traces the development of this mature sexual aim from infancy.

Freud describes how 'we see a great number of component instincts, arising from different areas and regions of the body, which strive for satisfaction fairly independently of one another', and how the pregenital phases of sexual life are dominated successively by the impulse to obtain satisfaction of the erotogenic zones of mouth, anus and phallus. 'These impulses which strive for pleasure are not all taken up into the final organization of the sexual function. A number of them are set aside as unserviceable, by repression or some other means; a few of them are diverted from their aim . . . and used to strengthen other impulses', then sharing their further vicissitudes.[3]

At puberty the genitalia develop into their mature form. Now, 'a new sexual aim appears, and all the component instincts combine to attain it, while the erotogenic zones become subordinated to the primacy of the genital zone . . .'

The new sexual aim in men consists in the 'discharge of the sexual products', to which the highest degree of pleasure is attached. 'The sexual instinct is now subordinated to the reproductive function; it becomes, so to say, altruistic.'[4] In women the aim becomes the stimulation of the erotogenic zone of the vagina.[5]

' . . . what were formerly self-contained sexual acts (satisfaction of erotogenic zones), attended by pleasure and excitation, become acts preparatory to the new sexual aim . . .'[6] If 'the fore-pleasure turns out to be too great and the element of tension too small . . . the preparatory act . . . takes the place of the normal sexual aim . . . such is . . . the mechanism of many perversions'.[7] If the aims of the component instincts are repressed they may find expression as symptoms. Also what one describes as a person's character is

[1] ibid., p. 184.
[2] (1905d) *Three Essays on the Theory of Sexuality*, S.E., Vol. 7, p. 149.
[3] (1933a) *New Introductory Lectures on Psycho-Analysis*, S.E., Vol. 22, p. 98 f.
[4] (1950d) *Three Essays on the Theory of Sexuality*, S.E., Vol. 7, p. 207.
[5] ibid., p. 221.   [6] ibid., p. 234.
[7] ibid., p. 211.

built up to a considerable extent from the material of sexual excitations and is composed of instincts that have been fixed since childhood, of constructions achieved by means of sublimation and of other constructions, employed for holding in check perverse impulses which have been recognized as being unutilizable.[1] In latency the sexual aim is 'mitigated' and represents 'what may be described as the "affectionate current" of sexual life ... behind this ... lie concealed the old sexual longings of the infantile component instincts which have now become unserviceable'.[2] This process was later termed 'inhibited in their aim'.[3]

An unpublished letter of Freud's dated 1909, makes it quite clear that he early on assumed there must be a fusion of aggression with the sexual instinct in order for the sexual aim to be achieved.

In the *New Introductory Lectures*, after he had formulated his theory of the two fundamental instincts of Eros and Aggression he describes how 'every instinctual impulse that we can examine consists of similar fusions or alloys of the two classes of instinct. These fusions, of course, would be in the most varied ratios. Thus the erotic instincts would introduce the multiplicity of their sexual aims into the fusion, while the others would only admit of mitigations or gradations in their monotonous trend'.[4]

The Sexual Object
Freud uses this term both in the sense of the 'thing in regard to which or through which the instinct is able to achieve its aim' and in the sense of the love object as a whole person. In the former sense the object 'is what is most variable about an instinct and is not originally connected with it, but becomes assigned to it only in consequence of being peculiarly fitted to make satisfaction possible. The object is not necessarily something extraneous: it may equally well be a part of the subject's own body. It may be changed any number of times in the course of the vicissitudes which the instinct undergoes ... '[5]

When 'the first beginnings of sexual satisfaction are still linked with the taking of nourishment, the sexual instinct has a sexual

---

[1] ibid., pp. 237–9
[2] ibid., p. 200.
[3] (1915c) 'Instincts and Their Vicissitudes', S.E. Vol. 14, p. 122, cf. also (1933a) *New Introductory Lectures on Psycho-Analysis*, S.E., Vol. 22, p. 97.
[4] (1933a) *New Introductory Lectures on Psycho-Analysis*, S.E., Vol. 22, p. 104 f.
[5] (1915c) 'Instincts and Their Vicissitudes', S.E., Vol. 14, p. 122 f.

object outside the infant's own body in the shape of his mother's breast. It is only later that the instinct loses that object . . . and becomes auto-erotic'.[1] Freud takes the example of thumb-sucking to show how 'the sexual activity, detached from the nutritive activity, has substituted for the extraneous object one situated in the subject's own body'.[2] He describes how 'infantile sexual life, in spite of the preponderating influence of the erotogenic zones, exhibits components which from the very first involve other people as sexual objects. Such are the instincts of scopophilia, exhibitionism and cruelty'.[3]

Freud quotes Abraham (1924) as showing how in the second phase of the anal stage 'consideration for the object makes its first appearance as a precursor of a later erotic cathexis'. And already, in the second oral stage (the oral sadistic) distinguished by the onset of biting activities, we get the first manifestations of ambivalence in the relation to the object.[4]

In tracing the development of object love, Freud describes how the mother or nurse through their care stimulate the child's erotogenic zones and in thus 'teaching the child to love' prepare him for the choice of an object.[5]

The 'efflorescence of infantile sexual life (between the ages of two and five) already gives rise to the choice of an object, with all the wealth of mental activities which such a process involves . . . in spite of the lack of synthesis between the different instinctual components and the uncertainty of the sexual aim . . . [this phase] must be regarded as an important precursor of the subsequent final sexual organization'.[6] The onset of sexual development is interrupted by the latency period.

In puberty comes the subordination of all other sources of sexual excitation under the primacy of the genital zones and the process of finding an object . . . this is based on the child's infantile 'sexual inclination towards his parents . . . but is . . . diverted away from them, owing to the barrier against incest . . .'[7] The infantile repressed currents and the new sensual current should converge, leading to 'the focusing of all desires upon a single object'.[8]

[1] (1905d) Three Essays on the Theory of Sexuality, S.E., Vol 7, p. 222.
[2] ibid., p. 198.   [3] ibid., p. 191 f.
[4] (1933a) New Introductory Lectures on Psycho-Analysis, S.E., Vol 22, p. 99.
[5] (1905d) Three Essays on the Theory of Sexuality, S.E., Vol. 7, p. 222 f.
[6] [1920] (1905d) Three Essays on the Theory of Sexuality, S.E. Vol. 7, p. 234.
[7] ibid., p. 235.   [8] ibid., p. 200

COMPONENT INSTINCTS

Definition

Component instincts is the term used to designate any one of several different elements which by coming together and organizing themselves in special ways, give shape to the final structure of the fully developed instinct. At the time these formulations were made Freud was referring specifically to the sexual instinct.

History

The theory of component instincts was first adumbrated in a letter to Fliess of December 6, 1896.[1] The term as such first appeared in the *Three Essays on the Theory of Sexuality*.[2] What is covered here refers mainly to the 'component instincts' of the 'sexual drive'.

The theory of 'component instincts' was derived from Freud's observation that the perversions are only made intelligible if the convergence of several motive forces was assumed: 'If such perversions admit of analysis, that is, if they can be taken to pieces, then they must be of a composite nature. This gives us a hint that perhaps the sexual instinct itself may be no simple thing, but put together from components which have come apart again in the perversions.'[3] 'A child's sexual life is indeed made up entirely of the activities of a number of component instincts which seek, independently of one another, to obtain pleasure, in part from the subject's own body and in part already from an external object.'[4]

In mature sexuality, some of the component instincts come to form part of what Freud named 'fore-pleasure', that is, when after having been predominantly autoerotic and pursuing—independently of one another—certain types of pleasure as their sole sexual aim, they become subordinated under the primacy of the genital zone. The danger implicit here is that these 'fore-pleasure' activities, due to the excitation of the erotogenic zones, can take

---

[1] (1950a[1887–1902]) *The Origins of Psychoanalysis, Letters to Wilhelm Fliess*, Imago, London 1954, pp. 73–81.
[2] (1905d) *Three Essays on the Theory of Sexuality*, S.E., Vol. 7, p. 166.
[3] ibid., p. 162.
[4] (1916–17) *Introductory Lectures on Psycho-Analysis*, S.E., Vol. 15–16, p. 316.

the place of the normal sexual aim or 'end-pleasure', that is, the pleasure derived from the sexual act.[1]

Their source
'What we have called the component instincts of sexuality are either derived directly from these internal sources [Freud here implies a great number of internal processes out of which sexual excitation arises as a concomitant effect, as soon as the intensity of these processes passes beyond certain quantitative limits] or are composed of elements both from those sources and from the erotogenic zones.'[2]

'What distinguishes the instincts from one another and endows them with specific qualities is their relation to their somatic sources and their aims. . . . There is a further provisional assumption. . . . It is to the effect that excitations of two kinds arise from the somatic organs. . . . One of these kinds of excitations we describe as being specifically sexual, and we speak of the organ concerned as the "erotogenic zone" of the sexual component instinct arising from it.'[3]

Order of emergence
In relation to the order of emergence of the component instincts Freud stated: 'The order in which the various instinctual impulses come into activity seems to be phylogenetically determined; so too, does the length of time during which they are able to manifest themselves before they succumb to the effects of some freshly emerging instinctual impulse or to some typical repression [meaning here defence]. Variations, however, seem to occur both in temporal sequence and in duration, and these variations must exercise a determining influence upon the final result.'[4]

Their objects
Freud expressed the view that 'infantile sexual life, in spite of the preponderating dominance of erotogenic zones, exhibits components which from the very first involve other people as sexual objects. Such are the instincts of scopophilia, exhibitionism and cruelty, which appear in a sense independently of erotogenic

[1] (1905d) *Three Essays on the Theory of Sexuality*, S.E., Vol. 7, p. 210 f.
[2] ibid., p. 205.   [3] ibid., p. 168.
[4] ibid., p. 241.

zones; these instincts do not enter into intimate relations with genital life until later, but are already to be observed in childhood as independent impulses, distinct in the first instance from erotogenic sexual activity'.[1] At a later stage Freud modified the formulation given above, partly no doubt on account of the theory of *narcissism*, which he had developed in the meantime. He says: 'For the beginning of its activity the scopophilic instinct is autoerotic: it has indeed an object, but that object is part of the subject's own body. It is only later that the instinct is led, by a process of comparison, to exchange this object for an analogous part of someone else's body.'[2]

Freud remarks how the activity of the component instincts are to start with autoerotic, 'their object is negligible in comparison with the organ which is their source, and as a rule coincides with that organ. The object of the scopophilic instinct, however, though it too is in the first instance a part of the subject's own body, is not the eye itself; and in sadism the organic source, which is probably the muscular apparatus . . . points unequivocally at an object other than itself, even though that object is part of the subject's own body'.[3] Freud further referred to the fact that the component instincts frequently appear as a pair of opposites, one representing the active and the other the passive part of the pair.[4]

Line of development from autoerotism to object-love
An important line of development to be followed by the component instincts goes from autoerotism to object love through primary narcissism.

'There comes a time in the development of the individual at which he unifies his sexual instincts (which have hitherto been engaged in autoerotic activities) in order to obtain a love-object; and he begins by taking himself, his own body, as his love-object [here Freud is referring to primary narcissism], and only subsequently proceeds from this to the choice of some person other than himself as his object.'[5]

One important source of confusion is due to not taking into

[1] ibid., p. 191 f.
[2] (1915c) 'Instincts and their Vicissitudes'. S.E., Vol. 14, p. 130.
[3] ibid., p. 132.
[4] (1910a) 'Five Lectures on Psycho-Analysis', S.E, Vol. 11, p. 14.
[5] (1911c) 'Psycho-Analytic Notes on an Autobiographical Account of a Case of Paranoia (Dementia Paranoides)', S.E., Vol 12, p. 60.

account the fact that Freud made it quite clear 'that the attitudes of love and hate cannot be made use of for the relations of *instincts* to their objects, but are reserved for the relations of the *total ego* to objects'.[1]

Component instincts and libidinal phases of development

The different component instincts can be observed in connection with the libidinal phases of development. Freud says: 'We must regard each individual as possessing an oral erotism, an anal erotism, a urethral erotism, etc., and . . . the existence of mental complexes corresponding to these implies no judgement of abnormality or neurosis. The differences separating the normal from the abnormal can lie only in the relative strength of the individual components of the sexual instinct and in the use to which they are put in the course of development.'[2]

Constitution and component instincts

According to Freud one can distinguish a number of constitutions according to the innate preponderance of one or the other of the component instincts.[3]

'The hereditary sexual constitution presents us with a great variety of dispositions, according as one component instinct or another, alone or in combination with others, is inherited in particular strength.'[4]

Clinical applications

Normality and neuroses are closely linked with the developmental vicissitudes of the component instincts. ' . . . the constitutional sexual disposition of children is incomparably more variegated than might have been expected, . . . it deserves to be described as "polymorphously perverse" and . . . what is spoken of as the normal behaviour of the sexual function emerges from this disposition after certain of its components have been repressed . . . *normality* is a result of the repression of certain component instincts and constituents of the infantile disposition and of the subordination of the remaining constituents under the primacy of the genital

---

[1] (1915c) 'Instincts and their Vicissitudes', S.E., Vol. 14, p. 137.
[2] (1905d) *Three Essays on the Theory of Sexuality*. S.E., Vol. 7, p. 205 n.
[3] ibid., p. 171.
[4] (1916–17) *Introductory Lectures on Psycho-Analysis*, S.E., Vol. 15–16, p. 362.

zones . . . *perversions* correspond to disturbances of this coalescence owing to the overpowering and compulsive development of certain of the component instincts . . . *neuroses* can be traced back to an excessive repression of the libidinal trends.'[1]

And:

'An especially prominent part is played as factors in the formation of symptoms in psychoneuroses by the component instincts, which emerge for the most part as pairs of opposites . . .'[2]

Vicissitudes

Freud described the possible vicissitudes of the component instincts. An instinct could be reversed into its opposite, that is, either a change from an active to a passive aim, for example, or on other occasions a reversal of its content (reaction formation); furthermore it could be turned round upon the self, repressed, sublimated, etc.[3] He further pointed out how certain traits of character, e.g. orderliness, parsimony and obstinacy, proceed from the dissipation of anal erotism and its employment in other ways, and how a similar connection exists between ambition and urethral erotism. Similarly other traits of character he thought would turn out to be either precipitates or reaction formations related to pre-genital libidinal formations.[4] 'In the same way, the pathogenic significance of the constitutional factors must be weighed according to how much *more* of one component instinct than of another is present in the inherited disposition.'[5]

---

[1] (1906a) 'My Views on the Part played by Sexuality in the Aetiology of the Neuroses', S.E., Vol. 7, p. 277.

[2] (1905d) *Three Essays on the Theory of Sexuality*, S.E., Vol. 7, p. 166.

[3] (1915c) 'Instincts and their Vicissitudes', S.E., Vol. 14, p. 126.

[4] (1933a) *New Introductory Lectures on Psycho-Analysis*, S.E., Vol. 22, p. 102 f.

[5] (1916–17) *Introductory Lectures on Psycho-Analysis*, S.E., Vol. 16, p. 384 f.

EROTOGENIC ZONES

1. Definition

An erotogenic zone 'is a part of the skin or mucous membrane in which stimuli of a certain sort evoke a feeling of pleasure possessing a particular quality. There can be no doubt that the stimuli which produce the pleasure are governed by special conditions, though we do not know what those are. A rhythmic character must play a part among them and the analogy of tickling is forced upon our notice. . . . There are predestined erotogenic zones, as is shown by the example of sucking. The same example, however, also shows us that any other part of the skin or mucous membrane can take over the functions of an erotogenic zone, and must therefore have some aptitude in that direction. Thus the quality of the stimulus has more to do with producing the pleasurable feeling than has the nature of the part of the body concerned. . . . Erotogenic and hysterogenic zones show the same characteristics.' [In a footnote added in 1915 he said: 'After further reflection and taking other observations into account, I have been led to ascribe the quality of erotogenicity to all parts of the body and to all the internal organs'].[1] 'We call the parts of the body that are important in the acquisition of sexual pleasure "erotogenic zones".'[2]

2. History

The first published use of the term *erotogenic zone* appears in the *Three Essays on Sexuality*, 1905. The conceptualization, however, was rather thoroughly developed in the years between 1896 and 1905[3] e.g. *Origins of P.A.*, letters 52, 55, and 75. *Jones* comments that the term *erotogenic zone* was 'undoubtedly coined on the model of the *hysterogenic zones*,' Freud noted that both types of zones shared the same characteristics.[4] The significance of erotogenic zones seems to have been elucidated from growing clinical ex-

---

[1] (1905d), *Three Essays on the Theory of Sexuality*, S.E., Vol 7, p. 193 f.
[3] (1910a) 'Five Lectures on Psycho-Analysis', S.E., Vol. 11, p. 44.
[2] (1950a [1887–1902]) *The Origins of Psychoanalysis*, p. 175 f., see also pp. 187 f., 232 f.
[4] Jones, E., *Sigmund Freud, Life and Works*, Hogarth Press, Vol. 2, p. 289 n.a. See also (1905d) *Three Essays on the Theory of Sexuality*, S.E., Vol. 7, p. 183 f.

perience with perversions, hysterics and the evidence of the universal, active sexuality of childhood.[1] It is a basic concept since it provides one of the links between biology and the libido and instinct theories of psychoanalytic psychology.

3. *Predestined erotogenic zones*
Certain zones or areas of the body are in effect predestined by their anatomical juxtaposition to vital organs as to receive stimuli. These erotogenic zones are the oral, anal, urethral, clitoral and genital zones. These predestined zones of erotization are linked to 'great organic needs' such that the satisfaction of the related biological drives produces the concommitant effect of stimulating the erotogenic zone.[2]

4. *Distinguishing characteristics of different zones*
Freud remarked that the clearest distinction between one zone and another concerns the nature of the contrivance required for the satisfaction of the instinct.

(a) *Oral zone.* In the case of the labial zone it consisted of sucking [what is here referred to as the labial zone was later subsumed under the oral phase of libidinal development and was further subdivided into (1) the sucking stage and (2) the biting stage. Freud is here referring to the first stage of later division.] and this will be replaced by other contrivances and muscular actions depending on the nature and position of the other erotogenic zones.[3] The labial (oral) zone is attached to the need for nourishment. Once the experience of pleasure has been established, as in sucking, it provides an impulse need for the repetition of the experience. This is manifest in a peculiar feeling of tension, of itching or stimulation which is centrally conditioned and projected on to the peripheral erotogenic zone.[4] The early establishment of oral eroticism provides the avenue for the infant to explore its body as in example via the inclusion of the thumb for pleasure sucking which establishes a second, though inferior erotogenic zone.[5] (See narcissism.)

(b) *The anal zone.* The anal zone is attached to processes of

---

[1] ibid., p. 289.
[2] (1916–17) *Introductory Lectures on Psycho-Analysis*, S.E., Vol. 16, p. 315 f.
[3] (1905d) *Three Essays on the Theory of Sexuality*, S.E., Vol. 7, p. 185.
[4] ibid., p. 184.   [5] ibid., p. 182.

elimination and excretion. In relation to the anal zone Freud said: 'It is to be presumed that the erotogenic significance of this part of the body is very great from the first'.[1]

(c) *The phallic zone.* The close connection of the glans and clitoris with micturition is evident. According to Freud they do not play the opening part and 'cannot be the vehicle of the oldest sexual impulses but are destined to great things in the future' . . . being the beginning of later normal sexual life.[2]

5. *The body as an erotogenic zone*
Other than the 'predestined zones', it was evident from the study of hysteria that 'any other part of the skin or mucous membrane can take over the functions of an erotogenic zone and must therefore have some aptitude in that direction'.[3] By 1914, Freud had concluded that one could regard 'erotogenicity as a general characteristic of all organs and [we] may then speak of an increase or decrease of it in a particular part of the body'.[4]

6. *The relationship between erotogenic zones and component instincts*
There is a close connection between the concept erotogenic zones and that of the component instincts. Freud assumed that in most cases a given component instinct did arise from a specific erotogenic zone. He suggested ' . . . that excitation of two kinds arise from the somatic organs, based upon differences of a chemical nature. One of these kinds of excitation we describe as specifically sexual, and we speak of the organ concerned as the "erotogenic zone" of the sexual component instinct arising from it.' One ought to be reminded here that Freud explicitly referred to the tentative nature of these formulations but as he pointed out: . . . 'if I omitted all mention of them, it would be impossible to say anything of substance about the instincts'.[5] In the *New Introductory Lectures* he referred to the theory of instincts as our 'mythology'[6] and described this type of discussion as 'biological psychology', that is the study of the psychological concomitants of biological processes.[7] Finally it is appropriate to note that according to Freud

[1] ibid., p. 185.
[2] ibid., p. 187.   [3] ibid., p. 183
[4] (1914c) 'On Narcissism', S.E., Vol. 14, p. 84.
[5] [1915] (1905d) p. 168.
[6] (1933a) *New Introductory Lectures on Psycho-Analysis*, S.E., Vol. 22, p. 95 f.
[7] ibid., p. 96.

each 'component instinct is unalterably characterized by its *source*, that is, by the region or zone of the body from which its excitation is derived'.[1]

Gratification of the erotogenic impulse/itching occurs in early infancy without regard to psychological objects and with no other 'aim' than extinction of the excitation.[2] With the maturation of the infant's psychical life, the impulses of the erotogenic zones, which had been capable of independent satisfaction, become organized with respect to an object in the external world which is needed to gratify the impulse.[3] (See *component instincts*, source, aim and object.)

7. *Sources of excitation in the erotogenic zones*
Excitation can be aroused by external sources, not least of which is the loving care of the mother which arouse excitation and provides gratification.[4] The erotogenic excitation may come either via internal stimuli incidental to general biological processes, or it may derive from external stimulation. But in both instances, the relief from excitation is to be found in yet another external stimulus or excitation which anomalously affords pleasure and gratification.[5] In time, the infant's affects and ideational processes will provide a third source of excitation. In all of these instances, gratification will be attended by manipulation/stimulation of erotogenic areas, by either child or external persons. Gratification is initially attained in each zone, such that oral, anal or urethral gratifications are not dependent on one another. Pubertal changes, however, mark a profound change both in the nature of the pleasure experienced[6] but also in the subordination of each zone to the dominant genital experience.[7] (See Libidinal Phase of Development.)

8. *Function of erotogenic zones after adolescence*
'The formula for the new function of the erotogenic zones runs therefore: they are used to make possible, through the medium of

[1] (1923a) 'Two Encyclopaedia Articles', S.E., Vol. 18, p. 256.
[2] (1925j) 'Some Psychological Consequences of the Anatomical Distinction between the Sexes', S.E., Vol. 19, p. 251.
[3] (1923a) 'Two Encyclopaedia Articles', S.E., Vol. 18, p. 256.
[4] (1905d) *Three Essays on the Theory of Sexuality*, S.E., Vol. 7, p. 223.
[5] ibid., p. 184.   [6] ibid., p. 210 f.
[7] ibid., p. 207. See also p. 235.

C

the fore-pleasure which can be derived from them (as it was during infantile life), the production of the greater pleasure of satisfaction.'[1] The danger implicit is that these fore-pleasure activities can take the place of the sexual aim and the pleasure of satisfaction and that is in fact what happens in many perversions [2]

9. *Erotogenic zones and constitution*
According to Freud 'it was possible to derive a multiplicity of innate sexual constitutions from variety in the development of the erotogenic zones . . . and that further help towards the differentiation of sexual constitutions may be found in the varying development of the individual sources of sexual excitation'.[3] Consequently everybody possesses oral, anal and urethral erotism, etc. The difference between normality and abnormality here can only lie in the relative strength of the individual components of the sexual instinct and in the use to which they are put in the course of development. In other words Freud took the view that there was another complementary series made out of the interaction between the innate sexual constitution and the environmental forces acting upon them.[4]

10. *Vicissitudes and clinical applications*
The erotogenic zones can suffer any one of several vicissitudes. The eroticism of the zones may become inactive with the transfer of libidinal cathexis to another zone,[5] because of maturational processes; because of repression and the reactive character traits that follow,[6] or because sublimation permits partial gratification via displacement.[7] The dominance of pregenital, erotogenic zonal excitation is characteristic of the perversions. Clinical work with hysterics most clearly demonstrated the remarkable plasticity of different zones and organs of the body to 'become the seat of new sensations and of changes in innervation'.[8] Freud has also referred to the pathogenic consequences of the erotization of both

---

[1] ibid., p. 211.
[2] ibid., p. 211.   [3] ibid., p. 205.
[4] [1920] ibid., p. 205 n.
[5] (1923a) 'Two Encyclopaedia Articles', S.E., Vol. 18, p. 256.
[6] (1908b) 'Character and Anal Erotism', S.E., Vol. 9, p. 45 f.
[7] (1933a) *New Introductory Lectures on Psycho-Analysis*, S.E., Vol. 22, p. 104 f.
[8] (1905d) *Three Essays on the Theory of Sexuality*, S.E., Vol. 7, p. 169.

ego functions and the functions of body organs.[1] 'Not only is a large part of the symptomatology of hysteria derived directly from expressions of sexual excitement, not only do a number of erotogenic zones attain the significance of genitals during neuroses owing to an intensification of infantile characteristics, but the most complicated symptoms are themselves revealed as representing, by means of "conversion", phantasies which have a sexual situation as their subject-matter.'[2]

[1] (1926d) *Inhibitions, Symptoms and Anxiety*, S.E., Vol. 20, p. 88. See also (1950d), p. 205 f.

[2] (1905d) *Three Essays on the Theory of Sexuality*, S.E., Vol. 7, p. 278.

EROTISM

SEE CONCEPTS: *Erotogenic zones, Component Instincts, Oral, Anal, Phallic, Genital Erotism*

In Freud's libido theory no distinction is made conceptually between sexuality and eroticism because genetically they stem from the same sexual instinct.[1]

The term 'eroticism' (or erotism) is used in reference to the excitations and gratifications connected with drive activity and experienced originally at certain *erotogenic zones* (see this Concept). It is used by Freud, and subsequently by other authors, usually coupled with an adjective denoting the specific zone referred to, viz. oral eroticism, anal eroticism, etc. These terms have acquired a wider connotation with the growth of clinical knowledge and psychological conceptualization in so far as they are also used to designate all kinds of derivatives, vicissitudes, developments arising from these originally zone-tied experiences (excitations, impulses, gratifications, activities) and the quantities of psycho-sexual energy involved; they refer as well to the respective phases of sexual organization dominated respectively by a 'leading zone' in childhood and to the respective component sexual instincts. (See appendix.)

History. The concept of erotism (although not used by Freud as a term, but referred to in the index as such) is foreshadowed in Freud's letters to Fliess[2] where, in letters, 54, 55, Freud refers to periodical dipsomania starting with diarrhoea or looseness '(N.B. the oral sexual system)' and says 'the dipsomania arose from the intensification (or rather substitution) of one impulse for the associated one'; in letter 75, 1897[3] dealing with perversions as due to excitations and stimulations of an oral and anal nature; in letter 141, 1901[4]: 'hysteria with tussis nervosa and aphonia, which can be traced back to pronounced sucking tendencies . . .'

---

[1] [1920 (1905d)] *Three Essays on the Theory of Sexuality*, S.E., Vol. 7, p. 197ff.
[2] (1950a [1887–1902]) *The Origins of Psychoanalysis*, London, Imago., p. 193 f.
[3] ibid., pp. 229–35.
[4] ibid., p. 327.

As far as can be ascertained, Freud used the term 'erotism' first in 'The Sexual Enlightenment of Children'.[1] 'This period of life [early childhood], during which a certain quota of what is undoubtedly sexual pleasure is produced by the excitation of various parts of the skin (erotogenic zones), by the activity of certain biological instincts and as an accompanying excitation in many affective states, is called the period of *autoerotism*, to use a term introduced by Havelock Ellis. All that puberty does is to give the genitals primacy among all the other zones and sources which produce pleasure, and thus to force erotism into the service of reproduction.'

In 1908, in 'Character and Anal Erotism' speaking of the connection between types of character and particular erotogenic zones he says 'the relation posited here between anal erotism and this triad of character traits',[2] and again in 1908 in 'On the Sexual Theories of Children' Freud states that the idea that a baby is got by a kiss betrays the predominance of *oral erotism*. He uses the term 'oral erotism' and 'anal erotism', etc., to denote the excitations arising from the erotogenic zones, the impulses, desires, activities pertaining to the component sexual instincts that are linked with body zones and functions and the pregenital phases of sexual development that are dominated by specific erotogenic zones.[3] In an addition made in 1920 to the *Three Essays on the Theory of Sexuality* Freud says ' . . . beginnings of an organization of the sexual instinctual components can be detected in the sexual life of children from its very beginning. During a first, very early phase, oral erotism occupies most of the picture. A second of these pregenital organizations is characterized by the predominance of sadism and anal erotism.'[4] On p. 239, in a footnote added 1920, Freud uses the terms 'anal erotism', 'urethral erotism' synonymously with the 'particular erotogenic components' and 'dispositions'.[5]

These uses of term are quoted *in extenso* to justify the meaning given above to the term 'erotism'. It seems that wherever in the *Three Essays* the terms anal or oral erotism, etc., are used, they occur in later additions to the original text but cover the totality

[1] (1908c) 'On the Sexual Theories of Children' S.E., Vol. 9, p. 133 f.
[2] (1908b) 'Character and Anal Erotism', S.E., Vol. 9, p. 175.
[3] (1908c) 'On the Sexual Theories of Children', S.E., Vol. 9, pp. 220–26.
[4] (1905d) *Three Essays on the Theory of Sexuality*, S.E., Vol. 7, p. 233.
[5] ibid., p. 239.

37

of insight gathered before then in regard to the characteristics of the erotogenic zones, the component sexual instincts and the phases of sexual development.

The widening of the concept to cover a variety of instinct derivatives is due to the evidence of plasticity of *erotogenic zones* (see this Concept) and their aptitude to substitute for each other in regard to gratification or excitation,[1] also to the fact that many other zones and organs of the body and functions can, via affective or thought processes of considerable drive cathexis become 'the seat of new (sexual) sensations and of changes of innervation', which accounts for a great variety of neurotic symptoms. (See *Erotogenicity* in concept *Erotogenic Zones*.)

Appendix

In psychoanalytic writings generally the terms 'orality', 'anality' are sometimes used synonymously with 'oral erotism', 'anal erotism' in the widened sense, in regard to body zones and to manifestations. Both kinds of terms have come to cover, apart from their original connotation as pertaining to specific component sexual instincts, a great variety of derivatives. They have become metapsychological concepts in the full sense. Writers other than Freud have applied the term 'erotism' also to various other body zones and functions such as 'muscle eroticism' etc., as well as auditory, skin, tactile and visual erotism.[2]

Other terms which refer to but should be distinguished from this concept include 'erotogenicity', which denotes the capacity of erotogenic zones (see this Concept) and, more generally, any part or organ of the body to send sexual excitations to the central nervous system. It should also be distinguished from 'phases of sexual development' and 'erotization'.

[1] ibid., p. 167.
[2] Sadger, quoted by Abraham, Karl, in *Selected Papers on Psycho-Analysis*, p. 238.

ORAL EROTISM

Introductory remarks. It is not easy to sort out priority in authorship between Freud and Abraham in regard to this concept and its various applications, clinical, characterological and in manifestations within the range of normality; the reason being that, after Freud had in the *Three Essays on the Theory of Sexuality* established the main thesis on the composite nature of the sexual drive(s) and their developmental sequence (1905, with additions 1915 and 1920) the close exchange of ideas between the two authors led to mutal fertilization in their later writings.

In 1905 Freud refers to the gratification experienced in sucking as a primary sexual gratification tied to the oral zone and linked with the function of nutrition, and the tendency to repeat such stimulation and gratification by autoerotic activity.[1] For this biologically and phylogenetically determined oral erotism, which is variable in strength[2] he stipulates a constitutional factor, which accounts for marked oral erotism both in infancy and later life: Persons with strong infantile oral erotism tend in adulthood to become 'epicures in kissing, inclined to perverse kissing, . . . have a powerful motive for drinking and smoking'.[3] Both for normal development and later pathological manifestations of oral eroticism an aetiological series of constitutional and developmental factors is postulated.[4]

Owing to reversibility of processes along the pathways leading from biological functions to sexual excitation disturbances affecting oral erotism may result in disturbances of the nutritional function.[5] Detachment of oral erotism from the feeding function 'becomes inevitable when the teeth appear' and food 'is also chewed up'.[6] In the latency period the sexual excitation produced by oral (etc.) eroticism provides a store of energy employed to a great extent for purposes other than sexual: (a) to contribute the

[1] (1905d) *Three Essays on the Theory of Sexuality*, S.E., Vol. 7, p. 179.
[2] ibid., p. 241.
[3] ibid., p. 182.
[4] [1920] ibid., p. 205.
[5] ibid., p. 204 f.
[6] ibid., p. 182.

sexual components to social feelings, (b) through repression and reaction formation to build up barriers against crude infantile impulses, i.e. an educational process leading towards limitation of oral-erotic manifestations in later life to what is considered normal at the expense of impulses that are considered perverse. A certain portion of infantile sexual impulses seems to evade these uses and appears as manifest sexual activity.[1] In puberty all oral sources of excitation become subordinated under the primacy of the genital zones and contribute to fore-pleasure in the sexual act.[2] The oral gratifications originally experienced in connection with sucking in of nourishment form the prototype of every later love relation. In a footnote added in 1915 this 'anaclitic' type of *object choice* is distinguished from the narcissistic type leading to pathological results.[3]

In regard to *Identification*: In additions made in 1915[4] Freud states that the sexual aim in the first oral or cannibalistic pregenital phase of sexual development, when sexual activity has not yet been separated from the ingestion of food, consists in the incorporation of the object—the archaic prototype of the mechanism of *identification*. Also in 1915, but somewhat later, in 'Instincts and their Vicissitudes' an ambivalent character is ascribed to the oral-erotic pre-stage of love in view of its aim to devour, descriptively to abolish the object.[5] A further statement to the effect that identification precedes object-cathexis and constancy occurs in *Group Psychology and the Analysis of the Ego*[6] in its archaic character of the first, oral-cannibalistic phase. In *The Ego and the Id*[7] Freud states that an important contribution of oral erotism, of an indirect nature, to character and superego formation occurs via the mechanism of identification or introjection 'which is a regression to the mechanism of the oral phase'. By the same mechanism the work of mourning is achieved.[8]

In regard to the fusion of sexual and aggressive drives: Freud in *Beyond the Pleasure Principle*[9] refers to the polarity between love

[1] ibid., p. 232.
[2] ibid., p. 234.   [3] ibid., p. 222.
[4] [1915] ibid., p. 198.
[5] (1915c) 'Instincts and their Vicissitudes', S.E., Vol. 14, p. 138 and n.
[6] (1921c) *Group Psychology and the Analysis of the Ego*, S.E., Vol. 18, p. 105
[7] (1923b) *The Ego and the Id*, S.E., Vol. 19, p. 28.
[8] (1917e) 'Mourning and Melancholia', S.E., Vol. 14, p. 251.
[9] (1920g) *Beyond the Pleasure Principle*, S.E., Vol. 18, p. 54.

and hate as object-directed erotic trends and states that 'during the oral stage of libido-organization the act of obtaining mastery over an object coincides with that object's destruction' while in his final conceptualization of the aggressive drives in terms of the death instinct he says that the fear of being eaten by the totem animal (the father) is ascribed to erotogenic masochism in its fusion with the libidinal impulses of the oral phase.[1] Freud sees the primitive root of important ego functions in oral-erotic impulses of introjection and ejection, as in the intellectual function of judgement and in reality testing.[2]

The influence of oral erotism on *sexual theories of children* and their pathogenic potentialities is discussed in 'On the Sexual Theories of Children'[3] and Freud states in general that such erroneous notions arise owing to 'the necessities of the child's psycho-sexual constitution',[4] and on childish fantasies as well as in mythology expressing ideas of the father devouring his son; *fears and phobias* in children and adults (of animals devouring or biting) are derivatives of non-oral instinctual desires, regressively expressed in oral-erotic terms[5] while the little girl's fears of being killed or devoured by the mother derives from (pre-verbal) oral and oral-sadistic trends towards the mother, and in both men and women these derivatives of early oral-erotic strivings later appear as transferred to the father.[6] The strong cathexis of the penis in later stages of sexual development 'has, in addition to its anal-erotic root, an oral one which is perhaps more powerful still: for when sucking has come to an end, the penis also becomes heir of the mother's nipple'.[7]

The role of oral erotism in normal adult manifestations
Freud refers to *Disgust* as a result of repression (reaction formation) in the oral zone and possible pathological significance[8] such as disgust experienced when kissed. Disgust of crude oral-erotic

---

[1] (1924c) 'The Economic Problem of Masochism', S.E., Vol. 19, p. 165.
[2] (1925h) 'Negation' S.E., Vol. 19, p. 237.
[3] (1908c) 'On the Sexual Theories of Children', S.E., Vol. 9, p. 223.
[4] ibid., p. 215.
[5] (1926d) *Inhibitions, Symptoms and Anxiety*, S.E., Vol. 20, p. 104, see also pp. 105, 108, 124.
[6] (1931b) 'Female Sexuality', S.E., Vol. 21, p. 227, see also p. 237.
[7] (1933a) *New Introductory Lectures on Psycho-Analysis*, S.E., Vol. 22, p. 101.
[8] (1905e[1901]) 'Fragment of an Analysis of a Case of Hysteria', S.E. Vol. 7, p. 30

gratifications in genital sexuality (fellatio or cunnilinctus) serves the restriction of the sexual aim and prevention of perversion, but may be overriden by libido.[1] Kissing is viewed as a legitimate and socially accepted fore-pleasure.[2] *Phrases* such as 'I could eat you up with love' show oral-erotic fantasies in normal adult sex relations. Similarly, an adult playing pretend-games with a child at being wolf or dog may pretend to 'gobble him up'. Usages of language, e.g. 'an appetizing' love-object, a 'sweet' person show the same. Symbolic representation in *dreams* are exemplified by sweet things and sweetmeat stand regularly for caresses or sexual gratification. Also referred to there is an anxiety belonging to the phase of oral erotism, which manifests itself (later) as a fear of death.[3]

Oral Erotism in clinical manifestations

In the Dora case there was intense activity at the oral-erotic zone at an early age which led to 'subsequent somatic compliance' and a disposition towards fellatio fantasies.[4] Nervous cough as a hysterical symptom is connected with fantasy of sexual gratification via the mouth.[5]

Female patients suffering from hysterical symptoms like eating disturbances, globus hystericus, constriction of the throat, vomiting, were found to have indulged energetically in sucking activities in childhood which were repressed later on.[6] Generally in psychoneurotics, and especially in hysteria, are found symptoms in which the mucous membrane of the mouth plays the role of the genital.[7] Such erotization leading to symptom formation and disturbances of organ function, exemplified by the mouth as an organ for kissing as well as for eating and speech, is generally responsible for disturbances of organ functions.[8] There is anorexia in young girls.[9] The Wolfman's eating disturbance represents regressively

---

[1] (1905d) *Three Essays on the Theory of Sexuality*, S.E., Vol. 7, p. 131 f.
[2] ibid., p. 150.
[3] (1918b [1914]) 'From the History of an Infantile Neurosis,, S.E., Vol. 17, p. 106 f.
[4] (1905e) 'Fragment of an Analysis of a Case of Hysteria', S.E., Vol. 7, p. 52.
[5] ibid., p. 47 f.
[6] (1905d) *Three Essays on the Theory of Sexuality*, S.E., Vol. 7, p. 182.
[7] ibid., p. 166, cf. p. 169.
[8] (1910i) 'The Psycho-Analytic View of Psychogenic Disturbance of Vision', S.E., Vol. 11, p. 214 ff.
[9] (1918c) 'On the Sexual Theories of Children', S.E., Vol. 9, pp. 106–8

his conflict over passive homosexual trends in his fear of being eaten by a wolf, the fixation point being in the phase of oral erotism with the cannibalistic aim of devouring.[1]

Perversions. Lips or tongue of one partner brought into contact with the genital of the other.[2]

Among male inverts there are 'restrictions of sexual aim—to the point of its being limited to simple outpourings of emotion—are commoner among them than among heterosexual lovers. Among women, too, the sexual aims of inverts are various: there seems to be a special preference for contact with the mucous membrane of the mouth'.[3]

The connection between melancholia and oral erotism was pointed out to Freud by Abraham in 1915, but before then Freud had already begun to see identification and introjection as deriving from oral erotism.[4] Abraham gives Freud credit for the first important step towards the discovery of the main mechanism operative in melancholia, viz. the psychic introjection of the lost object, while claiming for himself the discovery of regression to the 'oral or cannibalistic stage'. Freud states that a severely pathological outcome of such regression, if it goes with a withdrawal of libido is a state of narcissistic identification in which intake of food may be refused. He speaks in this connection of the 'still narcissistic oral phase of the libido' to which it regresses.[5]

[1] (1918b) 'From the History of an Infantile Neurosis', S.E., Vol. 17, p. 64, cf. p. 106 f.
[2] (1905d) *Three Essays on the Theory of Sexuality*, S.E., Vol. 7, p. 15.
[3] ibid., p. 145 f.
[4] (1917e) 'Mourning and Melancholia', S.E., Vol 14, p. 239 ff.
[5] ibid., p. 249 f.

ANAL EROTISM

Definition: Anal erotism comprises the drives characteristic of the anal phase of development when the anal zone is the leading one. There is erotism in connection with the act of defecation and also erotism in connection with activities such as anal masturbation and inversion. Interest is taken either in the act of defecation and the stimulation brought about to the mucous membrane lining the anus and anal canal or in the product of the act of defecation. While the erotism in connection with the act of defecation appears to be autoerotic, the way the individual deals with his sexual pleasure is object-related, and environmental and cultural factors are very significant, ' . . . the *sadistic* and *anal* impulses come to the fore, undoubtedly in connection with the appearance of the teeth, the strengthening of the muscular apparatus and the control of the sphincter functions.'[1]

' . . . Two stages can be distinguished in the sadistic-anal phase. The earlier of these is dominated by the destructive trends of destroying and losing, the later one by trends friendly towards objects—those of keeping and possessing. It is in the middle of this phase, therefore, that consideration for the object makes its first appearance as a precursor of a later erotic cathexis.'[2]

There is no final definitive statement as to whether or not Freud considered that urethral erotism was included in the concept of anal erotism or whether it required a separate phase. In one statement (that quoted on page 48 of this draft), urethral erotism is referred to in the paper on 'Character and Anal Erotism' (1908), implying that it is included under anal erotism. However, in a 1920 addition to the *Three Essays* (quoted in the last paragraph of this draft) urethral erotism is referred to as a separate phenomenon equal to the others.

Historical Development: Freud's earliest consideration of what was to be called the anal phase appears in the letter of 24.1.97 to Fliess, in the context of his insight into how medieval practices and religious rites paralleled the associations of his patients and their

[1] (1933a) *New Introductory Lectures on Psycho-Analysis*, S.E., Vol 22, p. 98.
[2] ibid., p. 99.

44

disturbances. 'I read one day that the gold which the devil gave his victims regularly turned into excrement; and next day Herr E., who reports that his nurse had money deliria, suddenly told me . . . that Louise's [the nurse's] money was always excrement.'[1]

In a later letter, quoted below, Freud, while developing the origins of the theory of 'repression', as then conceived of (but later termed 'reaction formation') referred to the erotic nature of the anal zone. He described the process by which formerly pleasurable sensations of smell became repellent. He cited the figure of speech 'He turns up his nose' which equalled that 'he regards himself as something particularly noble'. He went on: 'Now, the zones which no longer produce a release of sexuality in normal and mature human beings must be the regions of the anus and of the mouth and throat. This is to be understood in two senses: first, that the appearance and idea of these zones no longer produce any exciting effect, and secondly, that the internal sensations arising from them no longer make any contribution to the libido like the sexual organs proper. In animals these sexual zones retain their power in both respects; where they do so in humans the result is perversions.'[2]

In a 1919 addition to *The Interpretation of Dreams* Freud described how his patients revealed their anal birth theories through their dreams. 'We find an interesting link with the sexual researches of childhood when a dreamer dreams of two rooms which were originally one, or when he sees a familiar room divided into two in the dream, or vice versa. In childhood the female genitals and anus are regarded as a single area—the bottom.'[3]

Freud considered and wrote rather fully on the fact that jokes so frequently are concerned with the act and product of defecation, linking this with his research which showed this topic to have sexual connotations of varying intensities among normal people, especially children, as well as among neurotics. These statements and discoveries are accepted today but at the time they were put forth they were received with consternation and disbelief. Freud cited a series of verbal themes, all of which touched on anal material. For instance, 'Venus "Urinia"', though on the surface suggesting urine is a malapropism for "Urania", the heavenly, homosexual, love of

[1] (1950a [1887–1902]) *The Origins of Psychoanalysis*, London, 1954, p. 188 f.
[2] ibid., p. 231 f.
[3] [1919] (1900a) *The Interpretation of Dreams*, S.E., Vol. 5, p 354 f.

45

Plato's Symposium. "Gudel" was a real, aristocratic and wealthy Hamburg lady, to whom Hyacinth here gives the anal-sounding pseudonym of "Dreckwall". (Dreck = excrement.)[1]

In the 1905 edition of the *Three Essays* excitation of the anal zone was more fully described and understood and if one follows the various notes and additions to this work, it is clear now how the knowledge of this topic evolved and developed: 'The part played by the erotogenic zones is immediately obvious in the case of those perversions which assign a sexual significance to the oral and anal orifices. These behave in every respect like a portion of the sexual apparatus. In hysteria [they] . . . become the seat of new sensations and of changes in innervation . . . in just the same way as do the actual genitalia under the excitations of the normal sexual processes.'[2]

The following quotation from the 1905 edition of the *Three Essays* describes the erotogenicity of the mucous membrane lining the anal canal and the anus:

'Like the labial zone, the anal zone is well suited by its position to act as a medium through which sexuality may attach itself to other somatic functions. It is to be presumed that the erotogenic significance of this part of the body is very great from the first. We learn with some astonishment from psycho-analysis of the transmutations normally undergone by the sexual excitations arising from this zone and of the frequency with which it retains a considerable amount of susceptibility to genital stimulation throughout life.

'Children who are making use of the susceptibility to erotogenic stimulation of the anal zone betray themselves by holding back their stool till its accumulation brings about violent muscular contractions and, as it passes through the anus, is able to produce powerful stimulation of the mucous membrane. In so doing it must no doubt cause not only painful but also highly pleasurable sensations. One of the clearest signs of subsequent eccentricity or nervousness is to be seen when a baby obstinately refuses to empty his bowels when he is put on the pot—that is, when his nurse wants him to—and holds back that function till he himself chooses to exercise it. He is naturally not concerned with dirtying the bed, he is only anxious not to miss the subsidiary pleasure attached to

[1] (1905c) *Jokes and their Relation to the Unconscious*, S.E., Vol. 8, p. 79 n.1.
[2] (1905d) *Three Essays on the Theory of Sexuality*, S.E., Vol. 7, p. 169.

defecating. Educators are once more right when they describe children who keep the process back as "naughty".[1]

Freud goes on in this section to refer to anal masturbation and the erotic pleasures children experience in 'stimulation of the anal zone'.[2]

In the paper on 'Little Hans', the role of the child's fantasy and his identification with the mother are made very vivid, as is the pleasurable nature of the anal processes: ' . . . in little Hans's sexual constitution the genital zone was from the outset the one among his erotogenic zones which afforded him the most intense pleasure. The only other similar pleasure of which he gave evidence was excretory pleasure, the pleasure attached to the orifices through which micturition and evacuation of the bowels are effected. In his final fantasy of bliss, with which his illness was overcome, he imagined he had children, whom he took to the W.C., whom he made to widdle, whose behinds he wiped—for whom, in short, he did "everything one can do with children"; it therefore seems impossible to avoid the assumption that during the period when he himself had been looked after as an infant these same performances had been the source of pleasurable sensations for him. He had obtained this pleasure from his erotogenic zones with the help of the person who had looked after him— his mother, in fact; and thus the pleasure already pointed the way to object-choice. But it is just possible that at a still earlier date he had been in the habit of giving himself this pleasure autoerotically —that he had been one of those children who like retaining their excreta till they can derive a voluptuous sensation from their evacuation. I say no more than that it is possible, because the matter was not cleared up in the analysis; the "making a row with the legs" (kicking about), of which he was so much frightened later on, points in that direction.'[3]

In relation to the sexual use of the anal orifice Freud wrote the following:

'Where the anus is concerned it becomes still clearer that it is disgust which stamps that sexual aim as a perversion. I hope, however, I shall not be accused of partisanship when I assert that people who try to account for this disgust by saying that the organ

[1] ibid., p. 185 f.   [2] ibid., p. 187.
[3] (1909b) 'Analysis of a Phobia in a Five-Year-Old Boy', S.E., Vol. 10, p. 107 f.

in question serves the function of excretion and comes in contact with excrement—a thing which is disgusting in itself—are not much more to the point than hysterical girls who account for their disgust at the male genital by saying that it serves to void urine.

'The playing of a sexual part by the mucous membrane of the anus is by no means limited to intercourse between men: preference for it is in no way characteristic of inverted feeling. On the contrary, it seems that paedicatio with a male owes its origin to an analogy with a similar act performed with a woman; while mutual masturbation is the sexual aim most often found in intercourse between inverts.'[1]

In the paper on 'Character and Anal Erotism' (1908) Freud developed his increasing conviction of the connection between anal erotism and certain character traits of orderliness, parsimony (linked to the interest in the product of defecation) and obstinacy (connected with the act of defecation and the child's unwillingness to comply with the mother's wishes).

'Now anal erotism is one of the components of the [sexual] instinct which, in the course of development and in accordance with the education demanded by our present civilization, have become unserviceable for sexual aims. It is therefore plausible to suppose that these character-traits of orderliness, parsimony and obstinacy, which are so often prominent in people who were formerly anal erotics, are to be regarded as the first and most constant results of the sublimation of anal erotism.'[2]

Urethral erotism and its connection with ambition is first mentioned here. 'At present I only know of the intense "burning" ambition of people who earlier suffered from enuresis.'[3]

In the analysis of the 'Ratman' (1909) there are numerous examples of the way the patient's anal erotism contributed to his illness. Rats had many anal meanings. For instance, the rats meant money and also worms that bury in the anus; further 'the rat is a dirty animal feeding upon excrement and living in sewers . . .' These studies led to the conviction expressed in the paper on 'Character and Anal Erotism' which caused such indignation and astonishment when published.[4]

[1] (1905d) *Three Essays on the Theory of Sexuality*, S.E., Vol. 7, p. 152.
[2] (1908b) 'Character and Anal Erotism', S.E., Vol. 9, p. 171 f.
[3] ibid., p. 175.
[4] (1909d) 'Notes upon a Case of Obsessional Neurosis', S.E., Vol. 10, 213 f.

It was in the paper 'Disposition to Obsessional Neurosis' that Freud came to the conclusion that there is a pregenital sexual organization, and he used the term 'pregenital' here for the first time. At this period of development 'the component instincts have already come together for the choice of an object and that object is already something extraneous in contrast to the subject's own self, but in which *the primacy of the genital zones has not yet been established*. On the contrary, the component instincts which dominate this *pregenital organization* of sexual life are the anal-erotic and sadistic ones'.[1]

The special relation between anal erotism and obsessional neurosis is put forth here. Describing a female patient he wrote: 'The content of her obsessional neurosis was a compulsion for scrupulous washing and cleanliness and extremely energetic protective measures against severe injuries which she thought other people had reason to fear from her—that is to say, reaction formations against her own *anal-erotic* and *sadistic* impulses.'[2]

'But it is precisely in the field of character-development that we come across a good analogy with the case we have been describing —a confirmation, that is, of the occurrence of the pregenital sadistic anal-erotic sexual organization. It is a well-known fact, and one that has given much ground for complaint, that after women have lost their genital function . . . They become quarrelsome, vexatious and overbearing, petty and stingy; that is to say, they exhibit typically sadistic and anal-erotic traits which they did not possess earlier, during their period of womanliness . . . this alteration of character corresponds to a regression of sexual life to the pregenital sadistic and anal-erotic stage . . .'[3]

The sexual aim of anal erotism is here described as follows: In the place of the antithesis between male and female, as in the genital phase, the antithesis in this pregenital phase is 'between trends with an active and with a passive aim . . . Activity is supplied by the common instinct of mastery, which we call sadism . . . The passive trend is fed by anal erotism, whose erotogenic zone corresponds to the old, undifferentiated cloaca'.[4]

In a section added in 1915 to the *Three Essays* he wrote: 'A second pregenital phase is that of the sadistic-anal organization.

---

[1] (1913i) 'The Disposition to Obsessional Neurosis'. S.E., Vol. 12, p. 321.
[2] ibid., p. 320.   [3] ibid., p. 323 f.
[4] ibid., p. 322.

D

THE LIBIDO THEORY

Here the opposition between two currents, which runs through all sexual life, is already developed: they cannot yet, however, be described as "masculine" and "feminine", but only as "active" and "passive". The *activity* is put into operation by the instinct for mastery through the agency of the somatic musculature; the organ which, more than any other, represents the *passive* sexual aim is the erotogenic mucous membrane of the anus. Both of these currents have objects which, however, are not identical.

'This form of sexual organization can persist throughout life and permanently attract a large portion of sexual activity to itself. The predominance in it of sadism and the cloacal part played by the anal zone give it a quite peculiarly archaic colouring. It is further characterized by the fact that in it the opposing pair of instincts are developed to an approximately equal extent, a state of affairs described by Bleuler's happily chosen term "ambivalence".'[1]

In 1917 Freud interrupted a series of theoretical papers to publish a more clinical one on 'The Transformation of Instincts with Special Reference to Anal Erotism'. In it he deals with the problem of the 'later history of the anal-erotic instinctual impulses', and asks, 'What becomes of them when, owing to the establishment of a definitive genital organization, they have lost their importance in sexual life?' He then goes into the question of the complex unconscious relationships between the ideas of faeces, child and penis.[2] This 1917 paper is not the first discussion of these ideas which are already described in 1915 in the addition to the *Three Essays*. Some of the conclusions arise from the paper on the 'Wolfman' which was written shortly before, in which there is a considerable amount of material on this topic.

The Wolfman's preference for copulation from behind and his attraction to female buttocks were noted as being 'part of the fabric of the anal-erotic disposition'.[3]

In an addition of 1915 to the *Three Essays* the unconscious meaning of faeces is discussed:

'The contents of the bowels, which act as a stimulating mass upon a sexually sensitive portion of the mucous membrane, behave like forerunners of another organ, which is destined to come into

[1] [1915] (1905d) *Three Essays on the Theory of Sexuality*, S.E., Vol. 7, p. 198 f.
[2] (1917c) 'On Transformations of Instinct as Exemplified in Anal Erotism', S.E., Vol. 17, p. 127.
[3] (1918b [1914]) 'From the History of An Infantile Neurosis' S.E., Vol. 17, p. 41.

50

action after the phase of childhood. But they have other important meanings for the infant. They are clearly treated as a part of the infant's own body and represent his first "gift"—by producing them he can express his active compliance with his environment and, by withholding them, his disobedience. From being a "gift" they later come to acquire the meaning of "baby"—for babies, according to one of the sexual theories of children, are acquired by eating and are born through the bowels.'[1]

Similarly, Freud wrote in the paper on the Wolfman: 'Since the column of faeces stimulates the erotogenic mucous membrane of the bowel, it plays the part of an active organ in regard to it; it behaves just as the penis does to the vaginal mucous membrane, and acts as it were as its forerunner during the cloacal epoch. The handing over of faeces for the sake of (out of love for) someone else becomes a prototype of castration; it is the first occasion upon which an individual parts with a piece of his own body in order to gain the favour of some other person whom he loves. So that a person's love of his own penis, which is in other respects narcissistic, is not without an element of anal erotism. "Faeces", "baby", "penis" thus form a unity, an unconscious concept (sit venia verbo)—the concept, namely, of "a little one" that can become separated from one's body. Along these paths of association the libidinal cathexis may become displaced or intensified in ways which are pathologically important and which are revealed by analysis.'[2]

In a somewhat later paper, Freud states: 'Defecation affords the first occasion on which the child must decide between a narcissistic and an object-loving attitude. He either parts obediently with his faeces, 'sacrifices' them to his love, or else retains them for purposes of autoerotic satisfaction and later as a means of asserting his own will. If he makes the latter choice we are in the presence of defiance (obstinacy) which, accordingly, springs from a narcissistic clinging to anal erotism.

'It is probable that the first meaning which a child's interest in faeces develops is that of "gift" rather than "gold" or "money". The child knows no money apart from what is given him—no money acquired and none inherited of his own. Since his faeces are his first gift, the child easily transfers his interest from that

[1] [1915] (1905d) *Three Essays on the Theory of Sexuality*, S.E., Vol. 7, p. 186.
[2] (1918b [1914]) 'From the History of an Infantile Neurosis', S.E., Vol. 17, p. 84.

substance to the new one which he comes across as the most valuable gift in life . . .'[1]

The passage goes on to describe how the wish for the baby emerges from this as does the equation of faeces with penis—this is later described as follows:

'We have been able to study transformations of instinct and similar processes particularly in anal erotism, the excitations arising from the sources of the erotogenic anal zone, and we were surprised at the multiplicity of uses to which these instinctual impulses are put. It may not be easy, perhaps, to get free from the contempt into which this particular zone has fallen in the course of evolution. Let us therefore allow ourselves to be reminded by Abraham that embryologically the anus corresponds to the primitive mouth, which had migrated down to the end of the bowel. We have learnt, then, that after a person's own faeces, his excrement, has lost its value for him, this instinctual interest derived from the anal source passes over on to objects that can be presented as *gifts*. And this is rightly so, for faeces were the first gift that an infant could make, something he could part with out of love for whoever was looking after him. After this, corresponding exactly to analogous change of meaning that occur in linguistic development, this ancient interest in faeces is transformed into the high valuation of *gold* and *money* but also makes a contribution to the affective cathexis of *baby* and *penis*. It is a universal conviction among children, who long retain the cloaca theory, that babies are born from the bowel like a piece of faeces: defecation is the model of the act of birth. But the penis too has its fore-runner in the column of faeces which fills and stimulates the mucous membrane of the bowel. When a child, unwillingly enough comes to realize that there are human creatures who do not possess a penis, that organ appears to him as something detachable from the body and becomes unmistakably analogous to the excrement, which was the first piece of bodily material that had to be renounced. A great part of anal erotism is thus carried over into a cathexis of the penis. But the interest in that part of the body has, in addition to its anal-erotic root, an oral one which is perhaps more powerful still: for when sucking has come to an end, the penis also becomes heir of the mother's nipple.

[1] (1917c) 'On Transformations of Instinct as Exemplified in Anal Erotism', S.E., Vol. 17, p. 130 f.

'If one is not aware of these profound connections, it is impossible to find one's way about in the fantasies of human beings, in their associations, influenced as they are by the unconscious, and in their symptomatic language. Faeces—money—gift—baby—penis are treated there as though they meant the same thing, and they are represented too by the same symbols. Nor must you forget that I have only been able to give you very incomplete information. I may hurriedly add, perhaps, that interest in the vagina, which awakens later, is also essentially of anal-erotic origin. This is not to be wondered at, for the vagina itself, to borrow an apt phrase from Lou Andreas-Salome (1916), is "taken on lease" from the rectum: in the life of homosexuals, who have failed to accomplish some part of normal sexual development, the vagina is once more represented by it. In dreams a locality often appears which was earlier a simple room but is now divided into two by a wall, or the other way round. This always means the relation of the vagina to the bowel. It is also easy to follow the way in which in girls what is an entirely unfeminine wish to possess a penis is normally transformed into a wish for a baby, and then for a man as the bearer of the penis and giver of the baby, so that here we can see too how a portion of what was originally anal-erotic interest obtains admission into the later genital organization.'[1]

An important additional aspect was referred to by Freud in a note added to the *Three Essays* in 1920:

'Lou Andreas-Salome (1916), in a paper which has given us a very much deeper understanding of the significance of anal erotism, has shown how the history of the first prohibition which a child comes across—the prohibition against getting pleasure from anal activity and its products—has a decisive effect on his whole development. This must be the first occasion on which the infant has a glimpse of an environment hostile to his instinctual impulses, on which he learns to separate his own entity from this alien one and on which he carries out the first "repression" of his possibilities for pleasure. From that time on, what is "anal" remains the symbol of everything that is to be repudiated and excluded from life. The clear-cut distinction between anal and genital processes which is later insisted upon is contradicted by the close anatomical and functional analogies and relations which hold between them.'[2]

[1] (1933a) *New Introductory Lectures on Psycho-Analysis*, S.E., Vol. 22, p. 100 f.
[2] [1920] (1905d) *Three Essays on the Theory of Sexuality*, S.E., Vol. 7, p. 187.

While discussing obsessional neurosis Freud pointed out that: 'The chief task during the latency period seems to be the fending-off of the temptation to masturbate. This struggle produces a series of symptoms which appear in a typical fashion in the most different individuals and which in general have the character of a ceremonial. It is a great pity that no one has as yet collected them and systematically analysed them. Being the earliest products of the neurosis they should best be able to shed light on the mechanisms employed in its symptom-formation. They already exhibit the features which will emerge so disastrously if a serious illness follows. They tend to become attached to activities (which would later be carried out almost automatically) such as going to sleep, washing, dressing and walking about; and they tend also to repetition and waste of time. Why this should be so is at present not at all clear; but the sublimation of anal-erotic components plays an unmistakable part in it.'[1]

These changes were described as follows in a later paper: 'The development of civilization appears to us as a peculiar process which mankind undergoes, and in which several things strike us as familiar. We may characterize this process with reference to the changes which it brings about in the familiar instinctual disposi-tions of human beings, to satisfy which is, after all, the economic task of our lives. A few of these instincts are used up in such a manner that something appears in their place which, in an indivi-dual, we describe as a character-trait. The most remarkable example of such a process is found in the anal erotism of young human beings. Their original interest in the excretory function, its organs and products, is changed in the course of their growth into a group of traits which are familiar to us as parsimony, a sense of order and cleanliness—qualities which, though valuable and welcome in themselves, may be intensified till they become markedly dominant and produce what is called the anal character. How this happens we do not know, but there is no doubt about the correctness of the finding.'[2]

'A social factor is also unmistakably present in the cultural trend toward cleanliness. . . . The incitement to cleanliness originates in an urge to get rid of the excreta which have become disagreeable to the sense perceptions. We know that in the nursery things are

[1] (1926d) *Inhibitions, Symptoms and Anxiety*, S.E., Vol. 20, p. 116.
[2] (1930a) *Civilization and its Discontents*, S.E., Vol. 21, p. 96 f.

different. The excreta arouse no disgust in children. They seem valuable to them as being part of their own body which has come away from it. Here upbringing insists with special energy on hastening the course of development which lies ahead, and which should make the excreta worthless, disgusting, abhorrent and abominable. Such a reversal of values would scarcely be possible if the substances that are expelled from the body were not doomed by their strong smells to share the fate which overtook olfactory stimuli after man adopted the erect posture. Anal erotism, therefore, succumbs in the first instance to the "organic repression" which paved the way to civilization. The existence of the social factor which is responsible for the further transformation of anal erotism is attested by the circumstance that, in spite of all man's developmental advances, he scarcely finds the smell of *his own* excreta repulsive, but only that of other people's. Thus a person who is not clean—who does not hide his excreta—is offending other people; he is showing no consideration for them. And this is confirmed by our strongest and commonest terms of abuse. It would be incomprehensible, too, that man should use the name of his most faithful friend in the animal world—the dog—as a term of abuse if that creature had not incurred his contempt through two characteristics: that it is an animal whose dominant sense is that of smell and one which has no horror of excrement, and that it is not ashamed of its sexual functions.'[1]

To conclude: 'An inevitable consequence of these considerations is that we must regard each individual as possessing an oral erotism, an anal erotism, a urethral erotism, etc., and that the existence of mental complexes corresponding to these implies no judgement of abnormality or neurosis. The differences separating the normal from the abnormal can lie only in the relative strength of the individual components of the sexual instinct and in the use to which they are put in the course of development.'[2]

[1] ibid., p. 99 f., n.l.
[2] [1920] (1905d) *Three Essays on the Theory of Sexuality*, S.E., Vol. 7, p. 205 n.

PHALLIC EROTISM

1. *Definition*. Phallic erotism refers in general to the libidinal impulses whose source is the erotogenic zone of the penis or clitoris. It comprises more specifically the sexual impulses characteristic of the phallic stage of development when the penis or clitoris is the leading erotogenic zone, while the vagina has as yet little or no psychic significance for the child.

Nevertheless it ought to be noted that phallic excitation and masturbation are clinically observable in early infancy, i.e. in the stage of oral primacy. Freud distinguished between the masturbation of early infancy and the second phase of infantile masturbation, that of the phallic stage.[1] The first is autoerotic and seems to represent an overflowing of general excitation to the phallic zone: the second is related to the objects of the Oedipus complex, is accompanied by fantasies, and the impulses it discharges have specific aims, e.g. penetration, which the earlier phallic excitations may lack. We ought to note that Freud's usage of the concept of phallic erotism, after his paper 'The Infantile Genital Organization of the Libido' refers specifically to the sexuality of the phallic-oedipal stage.

Phallic erotism should furthermore be distinguished from genital erotism. The latter only arises at or after puberty when there is the biological possibility of discharge of semen and when vaginal orgasm supersedes clitoral orgasm. It would seem that the instinctual aims of phallic erotism are therefore somewhat different from the aims of genital erotism (e.g. there are phallic impulses to penetrate but not to discharge semen) even in the case of the boy where the same erotogenic zone remains dominant. 'It is not until development has reached its completion at puberty that the sexual polarity coincides with *male* and *female*.'[2]

II. *History of Concept*
Three phases can be seen in Freud's understanding of phallic

[1] [1915] (1905d) *Three Essays on the Theory of Sexuality*, S.E., Vol. 7, p. 188.
[2] (1923e) 'The Infantile Genital Organization of the Libido', S.E., Vol. 19, p. 145.

erotism. 1. In 1905, in the *Three Essays on the Theory of Sexuality*, Freud discussed phallic erotism simply as the manifestation of one of the several erotogenic zones of childhood. 'Among the eroto-genic zones that form part of the child's body there is one which certainly does not play the opening part, and which cannot be the vehicle of the oldest sexual impulses, but which is destined to great things in the future.'[1] He described how experiences of urinating and of being cleansed 'make it inevitable that the pleasurable feeling which this part of the body is capable of producing should be noticed by children even during their earliest infancy, and should give rise to a need for its repetition', which then leads to infantile masturbation.[2]

Furthermore, in 1905, Freud already denoted the clitoris as the female erotogenic zone in infancy, equivalent to the penis in the boy and had spelled out that consequently the little girl's genital sexuality was masculine in character. 'The autoerotic activity of the erotogenic zones is, however, the same in both sexes. . . . So far as the auto-erotic and masturbatory manifestations of sexuality are concerned, we might lay it down that the sexuality of little girls is of a wholly masculine character . . . it would even be possible to maintain that libido is invariably and necessarily of a masculine nature. . . .'[3] 'The leading erotogenic zone in female children is located at the clitoris, and is thus homologous to the masculine genital zone of the glans penis . . .' 'Puberty . . . is marked in girls by a fresh wave of repression, in which it is precisely clitoridal sexuality that is affected.'[4]

In discussing children's sexual theories, Freud also explained, in a 1915 addition to the *Three Essays on the Theory of Sexuality* that children make the 'assumption that all human beings have the same (male) form of genital'. Boys react to the discovery of sexual differences with the castration complex, while girls react with penis envy.[5]

2. In 1923, Freud wrote 'The Infantile Genital Organization: An Interpolation into the Theory of Sexuality', in which he established the phallic organization as a stage in the sequence of infantile libidinal development, following upon the oral and anal

[1] (1905d) *Three Essays on the Theory of Sexuality*, S.E., Vol. 7, p. 187.
[2] ibid., p. 188, and p. 233.
[3] ibid., p. 219.   [4] ibid., p. 220.
[5] ibid., p. 195.

57

stages. 'Even if a proper combination of the component instincts under the primacy of the genitals is not effected, nevertheless, at the height of the course of development of infantile sexuality, interest in the genitals and in their activity acquires a dominating significance which falls little short of that reached in maturity. At the same time, the main characteristic of this "infantile genital organization" is its *difference* from the final genital organization of the adult. This consists in the fact that, for both sexes, only one genital, namely the male one, comes into account. What is present, therefore, is not a primacy of the genitals but a primacy of the *phallus*.'[1]

'... *the significance of the castration complex can only be rightly appreciated if its origin in the phase of phallic primacy is also taken into acount.*[2]

In the *Outline* Freud re-stated the achievements of the phallic stage: 'In the early phases the different component instincts set about their pursuit of pleasure independently of one another; in the phallic phase there are the beginnings of an organization which subordinates the other urges to the primacy of the genitals and signifies the start of a co-ordination of the general urge towards pleasure into the sexual function.'[3]

3. A further enrichment of the understanding of phallic erotism came back with the work done in the twenties on 'Female Sexuality', (1931), 'The Dissolution of the Oedipus Complex' (1924), and 'Some Psychological Consequences of the Anatomical Distinction between the Sexes' (1925).[4]

III. *Phallic Erotism*: Aims

Freud does not characterize the phallic excitations of early infancy beyond saying that they are gratified by the infant's manual masturbation or thigh pressure.[5]

The phallic aims at the stage of phallic primacy are characterized as similar to masculine genital aims but this similarity is quali-

---

[1] (1923e) 'The Infantile Genital Organization of the Libido', S.E., Vol. 19, p. 142.

[2] ibid., p. 144.

[3] (1940a[1938]) *An Outline of Psycho-Analysis*, S.E., Vol. 23, p. 155.

[4] (1931b) 'Female Sexuality', S.E., Vol. 21. (cf. also (1934d), 'The Dissolution of the Oedipus Complex, S.E., Vol. 19, and (1925j) 'Some Psychological Consequences of the Anatomical Distinction between the Sexes', S.E., Vol. 19.

[5] (1905d) *Three Essays on the Theory of Sexuality*, S.E., Vol. 7, p. 188.

fied by the fact that the vagina has no psychic significance for the phallic child.

'Attached to this excitation [of the penis] are impulsions which the child cannot account for—obscure urges to do something violent, to press in, to knock to pieces, to tear open a hole somewhere.' But at this point the child is baffled in his attempts at imagining intercourse by his ignorance of the vagina.[1]

'... analysis leaves us in no doubt that the child's wishes extend beyond ... affection to all that we understand by sensual satisfaction—so far, that is, as the child's powers of imagination allow. It is easy to see that the child never guesses the actual facts of sexual intercourse; he replaces them by other notions derived from his own experience and feelings. As a rule his wishes culminate in the intention to bear, or in some indefinable way, to procreate a baby.'[2]

Thus, in Freud's description, phallic impulses do imply not only the wish to penetrate but the wish to create a baby, though perhaps in some more inchoate form than the genital impulses towards ejaculation. '... long-continued bedwetting is to be equated with the emissions of adults. It is an expression of the same excitation of the genitals which has impelled the child to masturbate ...'[3]

Like all libidinal components, phallic erotism can manifest both active and passive aims. If the active aims are to penetrate and to procreate, the passive aims are to be penetrated and to bear a baby. These passive aims are the basis, in the boy, of the negative Oedipus complex in which 'to be castrated' is a precondition of 'to be penetrated'[4] and may also be understood as being penetrated anally.[5] The wish to have the phallic zone stimulated by another person who thereby takes over the active role is also considered a passive phallic aim. Freud discusses this in connection with the girl's phallic relationship to the mother.[6] Perhaps this should be understood as the passive counterpart of the earliest infantile masturbation.

---

[1] (1908c) 'On the Sexual Theories of Children', S.E., Vol. 9, p. 218.
[2] (1926e) The Question of Lay Analysis, S.E., Vol. 20, p. 213.
[3] (1924d) 'The Dissolution of the Oedipus Complex', S.E., Vol. 19, p. 175.
[4] ibid., p. 176 (cf. also (1925j) 'Some Psychological Consequences of the Anatomical Distinction between the Sexes', S.E., Vol. 19, p. 249 f.
[5] (1918b [1914]) 'From the History of an Infantile Neurosis', S.E., Vol. 17, p. 78.
[6] (1931b) 'Female Sexuality', S.E., Vol. 21, p. 238.

This description of the active and passive aims of phallic erotism applies to girls as well as boys. In girls these are the aims of the phallic relationship to the mother which antedates the girl's positive Oedipus complex, and during which she for the most part fantasies the mother as a phallic object, i.e. endowed with a penis.[1]

The passive phallic aims of the little girl should not be confused with the passive aims of mature feminine genitality. In moving from the mother to the father as the oedipal object, the little girl takes a further step towards femininity in that she adopts a passive role. But the change in leading zones from clitoris to vagina does not take place until puberty. The girl's passivity towards the father still takes place within the horizon of the phallic world view: it means that she accepts her 'castration', and even wishes for castration or damage by the father, but she is as baffled as the boy in her struggle to comprehend the existence and nature of vaginal penetration. (Freud acknowledges clinical reports of the existence of vaginal sensations in infant girls, but says that even in such cases the clitoris remains the dominant erotogenic zone.)[2] Ideally, the girl's positive oedipal development means that the wish for a baby is firmly established as the successor of her wish for a penis, whereas in a boy the narcissistic evaluation of the penis should emerge dominant.

IV. *Phallic Erotism and the Oedipus Complex*
Phallic erotism during the phase of phallic primacy is object related: its objects are the objects of the Oedipus complex, and therefore the content of phallic erotism at this phase cannot be understood except in terms of the aims, wishes, and fantasies of the Oedipus complex. Though masturbation is the characteristic form of phallic gratification, it is not 'autoerotic', because in view of the accompanying fantasies, the child's 'masturbation is only a genital discharge of the sexual excitation belonging to the [Oedipus] complex, and throughout his later years will owe its importance to that relationship'.[3]

It may be said that, at least during the positive Oedipus complex of boys, the phallic stage represents a further development of the capacity for object relations over the relative object con-

---

[1] ibid., p. 238   [2] ibid., p. 228.
[3] (1924d) 'The Dissolution of the Oedipus Complex', S.E., Vol. 19, p. 176.

stancy of the anal-sadistic stage, because in the phallic stage, not only is there 'a sexual object and some degree of convergence of the sexual impulses upon that object,'[1] but a superseding of ambivalence, 'Because boys are able to deal with their ambivalent feelings towards their mother by directing all their hostility on to their father.'[2]

'This phallic phase ... is contemporaneous with the Oedipus complex ...'[3] In 'The Dissolution of the Oedipus Complex' (1924) Freud discussed how the existence of phallic primacy at this time determines the course of the conflicts of the Oedipus complex.

In the 1905 view of infantile sexuality, the Oedipus complex was seen as the final form of infantile object choice, but all the erotogenic zones were seen as participating equally in this attachment. In 'The Dissolution of the Oedipus Complex' Freud spells out the implications pointed to in his paper 'The Infantile Genital Organization of the Libido' as they refer to the Oedipus complex.

'*The significance of the castration complex can only be rightly appreciated if its origin in the phase of phallic primacy is also taken into account.*'[4] The threat of castration only takes on enough psychic impact to produce the castration complex at the phallic stage, because of the heightened narcissistic value of the penis at this time. Freud often described, from 1905 onwards, how the threat of castration is reinforced by the observation of the girl's lack of a penis. But the fact that castration becomes a psychic reality (for the boy as a real threat, for the girl as her image of her own genital), the fact that in the phallic stage 'the antithesis here is between having a *male genital* and being *castrated*',[5] is simply the reflection in the child's fantasy and thought of the nature of phallic erotism—namely that the erotogenic zone in both sexes is a 'masculine' one with characteristically masculine aims. The vagina does not exist for the child, not only because the child's researches are frustrated, not only because of lack of knowledge, as we see in 'enlightened' children or in those who have witnessed intercourse, but because their own (phallic) sexual experience gives

[1] [1924] (1905d) *Three Essays on the Theory of Sexuality*, S.E., Vol. 7, p. 199 n.
[2] (1931b) 'Female Sexuality', S.E., Vol. 21, p. 235.
[3] (1924d) 'The Dissolution of the Oedipus Complex', S.E., Vol. 19, p. 174.
[4] (1923e) 'The Infantile Genital Organization of the Libido', S.E., Vol. 19, p. 144.
[5] ibid., p. 145.

them no basis for comprehending the significance of the vagina.[1]

Freud's understanding of the existence of a phase of phallic primacy led him to weight the castration complex (i.e. castration disappointment) as the chief agent of the dissolution of the (boy's) Oedipus complex and the entry into latency—the inevitable frustration of oedipal wishes, and the possible phylogenetic patterning of latency in humans, taking a subsidiary place as causes of the entry into latency. 'Now it is my view that what brings about the destruction of the child's phallic genital organization is this threat of castration.'[2]

'This phallic phase . . . is submerged . . . and is succeeded by the latency period', by means of a partial repression of the Oedipus complex.[3]

V. *Phallic Phase and Female Sexuality*

In the papers dealing with female sexuality written after 1920, Freud amended his earlier view that the Oedipus complex in girls was simply the converse of the boys, and examined in detail the events of the female phallic phase. (1924) (1925) (1931). '*Whereas in boys the Oedipus complex is destroyed by the castration complex, in girls it is made possible and led up to by the castration complex.*'[4]

The castration complex in girls takes the form of penis envy, and it is penis envy (i.e. the recognition of both herself and the mother as 'castrated' beings, her disappointment and anger with the mother, and the narcissistic humiliation connected with clitoridal masturbation) which causes the girl to turn away from her first phallic love object, the mother. With this turning away 'there is to be observed a marked lowering of the active sexual impulses and a rise of the passive ones. . . . the active trends have been affected by frustration more strongly; they have proved totally unrealizable and are therefore abandoned by the libido more readily. But the passive trends have not escaped disappointment either. With the turning-away from the mother clitoridal masturbation frequently ceases as well; and often enough when the small girl represses her previous masculinity a considerable portion of her sexual trends in general is permanently injured too. The transition to the father-

---

[1] (1908c) 'On the Sexual Theories of Children', S.E., Vol. 9, pp. 215–25.
[2] (1924d) 'The Dissolution of the Oedipus Complex', S.E., Vol. 19, p. 175.
[3] ibid., p. 174.
[4] (1925j) 'Some Psychological Consequences of the Anatomical Distinction between the Sexes', S.E., Vol. 19, p. 256.

object is accomplished with the help of the passive trends in so far as they have escaped the catastrophe.'[1]

VI. *Associated Component Instincts*

The component instincts of exhibitionism and scopophilia are especially prominent during the phallic phase when they subserve and are coloured by the dominant phallic erotism.

Intense sexual curiosity is also characteristic in the phallic stage. It is provoked especially by the impact which the observation of sexual differences has on the phallic child, though the birth of a sibling before phallic primacy also may instigate 'the sexual researches of children'. Freud seemed to view this curiosity as an instinctual phenomenon arising from a component or an aspect of the phallic urges: 'The driving force which this male portion of the body will develop later at puberty expresses itself at this period of life mainly as an urge to investigate, as sexual curiosity.'[2]

VII. *Clinical Applications*

See Oedipus Complex.

[1] (1931b) 'Female Sexuality', S.E., Vol. 21, p. 239.
[2] (1923e) 'The Infantile Genital Organization of the Libido', S.E., Vol. 19, p. 143.

OEDIPUS COMPLEX

SEE CONCEPTS: *The Oedipus Complex of the Boy and The Oedipus Complex of the Girl*

The Oedipus complex is viewed by Freud as one of 'the corner-stones' of psychoanalysis.[1] The term appears to have been first used in his published writings in 1910.[2] However, the concept had been long familiar to him. The existence of the Oedipus complex was established in the summer and autumn of 1897. It was put forward in letters to Fliess.[3] In 1900, in *The Interpretation of Dreams*, Freud discusses the concept in relation to the connection between infantile sexuality and the legend of Oedipus but he does not in fact use the term 'Oedipus complex'.[4] The term 'Oedipus complex' was taken from the theme of Sophocles' play, 'Oedipus Rex'. It refers to the legend of the ancient king who unknowingly killed his father and married his mother, blinding himself as punishment. Freud comments that, 'we shrink back from him [Oedipus] with the whole force of the repression by which those wishes have since that time been held down within us'.[5]

'In the very earliest years of childhood (approximately between the ages of two and five) a convergence of the sexual impulses occurs of which, in the case of boys, the object is the mother. This choice of object, in conjunction with a corresponding attitude of rivalry and hostility towards the father, provides the content of what is known as the *Oedipus complex*, which in every human being is of the greatest importance in determining the final shape of his erotic life. It has been found to be characteristic of a normal individual that he learns to master his Oedipus complex whereas the neurotic subject remains involved in it.

' . . . Towards the end of the fifth year this early period of sexual

[1] (1923a) 'Two Encyclopaedia Articles', S.E., Vol. 18, p. 247.
[2] (1910h) 'A Special Type of Choice of Object made by Men', S.E., Vol. 11, p. 171 and n.1.
[3] (1950a[1897–1902]) *The Origins of Psycho-Analysis*, London, Imago, 1954, p. 207 and p. 223 f.
[4] (1900a) *The Interpretation of Dreams*, S.E., Vol. 4, p. 262.
[5] ibid., p. 263.

life normally comes to an end.'[1] 'This phallic phase, which is contemporaneous with the Oedipus complex, does not develop further to the definitive genital organization, but is submerged and is succeeded by the latency period.'[2] 'In the subsequent period of *puberty*, the Oedipus complex is revivified in the unconscious...'[3]

The term 'Electra complex', which Jung had used, was rejected by Freud because it was intended 'to emphasize the analogy between the attitude of the two sexes'.[4] 'I do not see any advance or gain in the introduction of the term "Electra complex", and do not advocate its use.'[5]

Freud stressed the contribution of bisexuality towards the more complete, twofold Oedipus complex, namely one which is both positive and negative. Still more important is the fact that Freud considered the strength of the masculine and feminine dispositions as chief determinants for the solution of the Oedipus situation: 'It would appear, therefore, that in both sexes the relative strength of the masculine and feminine sexual dispositions is what determines whether the outcome of the Oedipus situation shall be an identification with the father or with the mother. This is one of the ways in which bisexuality takes a hand in the subsequent vicissitudes of the Oedipus complex.'[6] And again: 'The relative intensity of the two identifications in any individual will reflect the preponderance in him of one or other of the two sexual dispositions.'[7]

Because there is therefore a positive and negative relationship for both the boy and the girl to each parent the Oedipal relationship may be seen as a quadruple one.[8] It was Freud's opinion that it was advisable to assume the existence of this quadruple situation: 'Analytic experience then shows that in a number of cases one or the other constituent disappears, except for barely distinguishable traces; so that the result is a series with the normal positive Oedipus complex at one end and the inverted negative one at the other, while its intermediate members exhibit

[1] (1923a) 'Two Encyclopaedia Articles', S.E., Vol. 18, p. 245 f.
[2] (1924d) 'The Dissolution of the Oedipus Complex', S.E., Vol. 19, p. 174.
[3] (1923a) 'Two Encyclopaedia Articles', S.E., Vol. 18, p. 246.
[4] (1931b) 'Female Sexuality', S.E., Vol. 21, p. 229.
[5] (1920a) 'The Psychogenesis of a Case of Female Homosexuality,' S.E., Vol. 18, p. 155, n.
[6] (1923b) *The Ego and the Id*, S.E., Vol. 19, p. 33.
[7] ibid., p. 34.   [8] ibid., p. 33.

the complete form with one or other of its two components preponderating.'[1] Though to start with it was assumed that the Oedipus complex was an identical development in the case of boys and girls (with the necessary changes in the role of each parent according to the sex of the child) later on Freud described the great differences between the Oedipus complex in the boy and the girl.

[1] ibid., pp. 33–4.

THE OEDIPUS COMPLEX OF THE GIRL

For some time Freud assumed that the sexual development in boys and girls was similar. In *The Interpretation of Dreams* he states that 'a girl's first affection is for her father and a boy's first childish desires are for his mother'.[1] This view changed in his paper on 'A Child is Being Beaten' (1919),[2] and from there onward the differences in the development of boys and girls are more and more clarified as Freud gained further insight into them. But still in 1924 Freud maintained that the 'girl's Oedipus complex is much simpler than that of the small bearer of the penis; in my experience, it seldom goes beyond the taking of her mother's place and the adopting of a feminine attitude towards her father.'[3] Later formulations suggest, however, that Freud came to regard the Oedipus complex in the girl as a much more complicated process. In 1935, for instance, he remarked on the fact that the little girl not only has to change her sexual object—from the woman (mother) to the man (father)—but her leading genital zone as well—from the clitoris to the vagina—in sharp contradistinction from the little boy whose sexual development is much simpler. His leading genital zone remains the phallus and the sexual object a woman.[4]

As Strachey points out, 'It was not until nearly the end of his life that Freud (in Section III of his paper on "Female Sexuality", 1931b) explained that these fantasies of his patients had in fact originally been connected not with their father but with their mother'.[5] In the same paper Freud further remarked that he was struck by the fact 'that where the woman's attachment to her father was particularly intense, analysis showed that it had been preceded by a phase of exclusive attachment to her mother which had been equally intense and passionate.'[6] Freud came to view the stories of seduction by the father as typical fantasies belonging

[1] (1900a) *The Interpretation of Dreams*, S.E., Vol. 4, p. 257.
[2] (1919e) 'A Child is Being Beaten', S.E., Vol. 17.
[3] (1924d) 'The Dissolution of the Oedipus Complex', S.E., Vol. 19, p. 178.
[4] (1935a) Postscript (1935) to *An Autobiographical Study*, S.E., Vol. 20, p. 36.
[5] ibid., p. 34.
[6] (1931b) 'Female Sexuality', S.E., Vol. 21, p. 225.

to the Oedipal phase, the source of which was the girl's relation to her mother, induced by excitation from the mother's early bodily care in the cleansing of the genital area.[1]

By now, Freud has reversed the view which he had held in 1900. Now we read: 'A female's first object, too, must be her mother: the primary conditions for a choice of object are, of course, the same for all children.'[2] The *duration* of this attachment had also been greatly underestimated. In several cases it lasted until well into the fourth year—in one case into the fifth year—so that it covered by far the longer part of the period of early sexual efflorescence. Indeed, we had to reckon with the possibility that a number of women remain arrested in their original attachment to their mother and never achieve a true changeover towards men. This being so, the pre-Oedipus phase in women gains an importance which we have not attributed to it hitherto'.[3]

Freud then indicates that this period cannot really be considered as pre-Oedipal but forms an essential part of the Oedipal phase itself which he calls the 'negative complex' here. What is not made fully clear is how this differs from the 'negative complex' which is part of the earlier formulations concerning the Oedipus complex in which both girl and boy will experience it as 'twofold, positive and negative . . . due to the bisexuality originally present in children'.[4] He presented the discovery as coming 'to us as a surprise, like the discovery, in another field, of the Minoan-Mycenean civilization behind the civilization of Greece'; it seemed 'so difficult to grasp in analysis'. He presented the view as follows. 'Since this phase allows room for all the fixations and repressions from which we trace the origin of the neuroses, it would seem as though we must retrace the universality of the thesis that the Oedipus complex is the nucleus of the neuroses. But if anyone feels reluctant about making this correction, there is no need for him to do so. On the one hand, we can extend the content of the Oedipus complex to include all the child's relations to both parents; or, on the other, we can take due account of our new findings by saying that the female only reaches the normal positive Oedipus situation after she has surmounted a period before it that is governed by the negative complex. And indeed during that phase a

[1] ibid., p. 238.
[2] ibid., p. 228.   [3] ibid., p. 226.
[4] (1923b) *The Ego and the Id*, S.E., Vol. 19, p. 33.

little girl's father is not much else for her than a troublesome rival, although her hostility towards him never reaches the pitch which is characteristic of boys.'[1]

It would appear, then, that some confusion may have resulted from the fact that Freud referred to this stage as pre-Oedipal in some instances and in others as part of the Oedipal phase. He furthermore points to a difference from the development of the boy in showing that for the girl the mother relation includes a hostility that 'is not a consequence of the rivalry implicit in the Oedipus complex, but originates from the preceding phase and has merely been reinforced and exploited in the Oedipus situation'. This accounts for the fact that, 'With many women we have the impression that their years of maturity are occupied by a struggle with their husband, just as their youth was spent in a struggle with their mother'.[2]

In addition to the differences pointed to above there is the further difference between the development of the girl and the boy in terms of the erotogenic zones involved: 'A man, after all, has only one leading sexual zone, one sexual organ, whereas a woman has two: the vagina—the female organ proper—and the clitoris, which is analogous to the male organ. We believe we are justified in assuming that for many years the vagina is virtually non-existent and possibly does not produce sensations until puberty. It is true that recently an increasing number of observers report that vaginal impulses are present even in these early years. In women, therefore, the main genital occurrences of childhood must take place in relation to the clitoris. Their sexual life is regularly divided into two phases, of which the first has a masculine character, while only the second is specifically feminine. Thus in female development there is a process of transition from the one phase to the other, to which there is nothing analogous in the male. A further complication arises from the fact that the clitoris, with its virile character, continues to function in later female sexual life in a manner which is very variable and which is certainly not yet satisfactorily understood.'[3] A somewhat later formulation suggests that the differentiation between clitoridal and vaginal sexuality must have contributed to the clear distinction between a phallic phase on the one hand and a genital one on the other. Freud

[1] (1931b) 'Female Sexuality', S.E., Vol. 21, p. 226.
[2] ibid., p. 231.   [3] ibid., p. 228.

69

writes: 'Thirdly comes the *phallic* phase in which in both sexes the male organ (and what corresponds to it in girls) attains an importance which can no longer be overlooked. We have reserved the name of *genital* phase for the definitive sexual organization which is established after puberty and in which the female genital organ for the first time meets with the recognition which the male one acquired long before.'[1]

Parallel with this first great difference (in zone) there is the other, concerned with the finding of the object. The girl must have her mother as first object like the boy, but 'at the end of her development, her father—a man—should have become her new love-object. In other words, to the change in her own sex there must correspond a change in the sex of her object.[2] . . . there is yet another difference between the sexes . . . It is only in the male child that we find the fateful combination of love for the one parent and simultaneous hatred for the other as rival'.[3]

'*Whereas in boys the Oedipus complex is destroyed by the castration complex, in girls it is made possible and led up to by* [it] . . . the castration complex . . . inhibits and limits masculinity and encourages femininity'.[4] The first step in the phallic phase is a 'momentous discovery' of the male organ. The little girl 'fall(s) a victim to envy' . . . 'She has seen it and knows that she is without it and wants to have it. . . .'[5] This has been named the 'masculinity complex' of women. Following this discovery the girl will at first deny it, keeping her fantasy of the hidden penis, or the hope of getting one later. She develops a 'sense of inferiority'. Penis envy may be displaced and persist as the character trait of jealousy. She may 'share the contempt' for women . . . and at least in holding that opinion, insist on being like a man. In consequence the girl's tie to the mother (who is held responsible for the lack of the penis) may be loosened.[6] At the same time the narcissistic wound of the discovery of her lack of a penis tends to bring about the giving up of clitoridal sexuality for the development of femininity. The explanation of the little girl's fight against masturbation can be seen in her 'narcissistic sense of humiliation' at the lack of the

---

[1] (1933a) *New Introductory Lectures on Psycho-Analysis*, S.E., Vol. 22, p. 98 f.
[2] (1931b) 'Female Sexuality', S.E., Vol. 21, p. 228.
[3] ibid., p. 229.
[4] (1925j) 'Some Psychological Consequences of the Anatomical Distinction between the Sexes', S.E., Vol. 19, p. 256.
[5] ibid., p. 252. [6] ibid., pp. 253–5.

penis. It is only at this point that the Oedipus complex begins to play its part. Now 'the girl's libido slips into a new position along the line . . . of the equation "penis-child" ', and for purposes of getting a child she now takes her father as love object and the mother becomes the object of her jealousy. She turns to her father and this attraction to him is secondary to her wish to obtain a baby from him.[1] In her disappointment in the father the little girl may return to the mother.[2] Or after relinquishing her father as love object, she may bring her masculinity into prominence and identify herself with her father (the lost object) instead of with her mother.[3] Freud places part of the outcome of object choice to the relative strength of masculine and feminine sexual dispositions.[4] It is easier to observe the possibility of alternative identifications with the parent of both sexes in girls than in boys.[5] 'Bisexuality . . . comes to the fore much more clearly in women than men.'[6]

Whereas in boys the Oedipus complex is 'smashed to pieces', in girls it escapes this fate, ' . . . it may be slowly abandoned or dealt with by repression, or its effects may persist far into women's normal mental life'.[7]

Freud described how, out of the acknowledgement of her castration, the little girl can take one of three lines of development. The first is a general revulsion from sexuality, and the second leads her to cling with defiant self-assertiveness to her threatened masculinity, clinging to the hope of getting a penis and the fantasy of being a man (Masculinity Complex). The third path leads to the final normal female attitude: 'Only if her development follows the third, very circuitous, path does she reach the final normal female attitude, in which she takes her father as her object and so finds her way to the feminine form of the Oedipus complex. . . . It is not destroyed, but created, by the influence of castration; it escapes the strongly hostile influences which, in the male, have a destructive effect on it, and indeed it is too often not surmounted by the female at all.'[8] Freud considered this as the chief reason for the

---

[1] ibid., p. 256.
[2] (1931b) 'Female Sexuality', S.E., Vol. 21, p. 241.
[3] (1923b) *The Ego and the Id*, S.E., Vol. 19, p. 32.
[4] ibid., p. 33.   [5] ibid., p. 32.
[6] (1931b) 'Female Sexuality', S.E., Vol. 21, p. 227 f.
[7] (1925j) 'Some Psychological Consequences of the Anatomical Distinction between the Sexes', S.E., Vol. 19, p. 257.
[8] (1931b) 'Female Sexuality', S.E., Vol. 21, p. 230.

fact that, in his view, women do not develop the quality of superego standards that men do.

Freud refers to a further difference in the development of boys and girls which may contribute to the different vicissitudes of the Oedipus complex in the two sexes. He states, with regard to the development of girls, that the 'lesser strength of the sadistic contribution to her sexual instinct, which we may no doubt connect to the stunted growth of her penis, makes it easier in her case for the direct sexual trends to be transformed into the aim-inhibited trends of an affectionate kind',[1] but he considered that in general insight was 'unsatisfactory, incomplete and vague' on this subject.

[1] (1924d) 'The Dissolution of the Oedipus Complex', S.E., Vol. 19, p. 178.

THE OEDIPUS COMPLEX OF THE BOY

In the boy, the *origin* of the Oedipus Complex is described by Freud as follows: 'the little boy develops an object-cathexis for his mother, which originally related to the mother's breast and is the prototype of an object choice on the anaclitic model; the boy deals with his father by identifying himself with him.'[1] The father is taken as his ideal.[2] 'For a time these two relationships proceed side by side, until the boy's sexual wishes in regard to his mother become more intense and his father is perceived as an obstacle to them; from this the Oedipus complex originates.'[3]

The *simple positive* Oedipus complex then develops. 'His identification with his father then takes on a hostile colouring and changes into a wish to get rid of his father in order to take his place with his mother. Henceforward his relation to his father is ambivalent; it seems as if the ambivalence inherent in the identification from the beginning had become manifest. An ambivalent attitude to his father and an object-relation of a solely affectionate kind to his mother make up the content of the simple positive Oedipus complex in a boy.'[4]

Apart from the simple positive Oedipus complex described above, the boy, due to the important role bisexuality plays in the Oedipus complex, 'also behaves like a girl and displays an affectionate feminine attitude towards his father and a corresponding jealousy and hostility towards his mother.'[5]

The *dissolution* and abolition of the Oedipus complex partly results from its lack of success, but primarily because of the threat of castration, heightened by the sight of the female genitals.[6] Freud first considered it to be repressed but later added (1924) that the process 'is more than a repression. It is equivalent, if it is ideally carried out, to a destruction and an abolition of the complex'.[7]

The Oedipus complex is destroyed because the child views either

---

[1] (1923b) *The Ego and the Id*, S.E., Vol. 19, p. 31.
[2] (1921c) *Group Psychology and the Analysis of the Ego*, S.E., Vol. 18, p. 105.
[3] (1923b) *The Ego and the Id*, S.E., Vol. 19, p. 31 f.
[4] ibid., p. 32.   [5] ibid., p. 33 f.
[6] (1924d) 'The Dissolution of the Oedipus Complex', S.E., Vol. 19, p. 173–75.
[7] ibid., p. 177. See also, Jones, Vol. III, p. 280.

the positive (active) or negative (passive) as a threat to his penis. The positive Oedipal complex entail the loss of the penis as a punishment and in the negative one its loss is a precondition to the wish to be taken as sexual object by the father. 'If the satisfaction of love in the field of the Oedipus complex is to cost the child his penis, a conflict arises between his narcissistic interest in that part of the body and the libidinal cathexis of the parental object.' The first force normally triumphs, the libidinal object cathexes are given up and replaced by identification,[1] either with the mother or intensification of the identification with his father. The latter is of course regarded as more normal as it consolidates the masculinity in the boy's character.[2] Libidinal trends are in part desexualized and sublimated and in part inhibited and changed into impulses of affection.[3] This leads to the creation of the superego and this initiates all the processes that are designed to make the individual find his place in the cultural community.[4] An important effect on the ending of the Oedipus complex on the boy is 'a certain amount of disparagement in the attitude towards women, whom (he) regards as being castrated'. This can lead to inhibition in the choice of object and if it is supported by organic factors to exclusive homosexuality.[5]

[1] ibid., p. 176.
[2] (1923b) *The Ego and the Id*, S.E., Vol. 19, p. 31 f.
[3] (1924d) 'The Dissolution of the Oedipus Complex', S.E., Vol. 19, p. 177.
[4] (1931b) 'Female Sexuality', S.E. Vol. 21, p. 229.
[5] ibid., p. 229.

DISSOLUTION OF THE OEDIPUS COMPLEX

SEE CONCEPTS: *Oedipus Complex, Latency, Puberty, Phallic Erotism, Genital Phase*

I. *Definition*

'The dissolution of the Oedipus complex' refers to a type of outcome or resolution of the oedipal conflicts which Freud explicitly conceived of as both an 'ideal' model and as typical of 'normal', non-neurotic development. According to Freud's final formulations, it should occur in the male child as part of the transition from the phallic-oedipal phase to latency, i.e. about the age of five years. The difference between male and female development in this respect is discussed below.

Freud summarized the psychic changes comprised in this process as follows:

'The object-cathexes are given up and replaced by identifications. The authority of the father or the parents is introjected into the ego, and there it forms the nucleus of the superego, which takes over the severity of the father and perpetuates his prohibition against incest, and so secures the ego from the return of the libidinal object-cathexis. The libidinal trends belonging to the Oedipus complex are in part desexualized and sublimated (a thing which probably happens with every transformation into an identification) and in part inhibited in their aim and transformed into impulses of affection. . . . This process ushers in the latency period . . .'[1]

The essence of this concept of the 'dissolution' of the Oedipus complex lies in the idea that the instinctual aims and object-cathexes of the Oedipus complex ceases to exist, even in the id.

The process we have described is more than a repression. 'It is equivalent, if it is ideally carried out, to a destruction and an abolition of the complex. We may plausibly assume that we have here come upon the borderline—never a very sharply drawn one—between the normal and the pathological. If the ego has in fact not

[1] (1924d) 'The Dissolution of the Oedipus Complex', S.E., Vol. 19, p. 176-7.

achieved much more than a *repression* of the complex, the latter persists in an unconscious state in the id and will later manifest its pathogenic effect.'[1]

'In boys ... the complex is not simply repressed, it is literally smashed to pieces by the shock of threatened castration. Its libidinal cathexes are abandoned, desexualized and in part sublimated; its objects are incorporated into the ego, where they form the nucleus of the superego. . . . In normal, or it is better to say, in ideal cases, the Oedipus complex exists no longer, even in the unconscious; the superego has become its heir.'[2]

II. *The History of the Concept*

In the 1905 edition of the *Three Essays on the Theory of Sexuality*, infantile sexuality was seen as primarily autoerotic, and the development of the 'incestuous object choice' seen as a feature of puberty. The phenomenon of latency was viewed as 'organically determined and fixed by heredity',[3] and not linked with the oedipal conflicts. The 1915 emendations gave recognition to the existence of 'infantile object choice' but still stressed puberty as the period in which the detachment of the libido from the infantile objects takes place.

' ... the diphasic nature of object-choice comes down in essentials to not more than the operation of the latency period. . . . The resultants of infantile object choice ... either persist as such or are revived at the actual time of puberty. But as a consequence of the repression which has developed between the two phases they prove unutilizable. Their sexual aims have become mitigated and they now represent what may be described as the "affectionate current" of sexual life. . . . The object-choice of the pubertal period is obliged to dispense with the objects of childhood and to start afresh as a "sensual current". Should these two currents fail to converge, the result is often that one of the ideals of sexual life, the focusing of all desires upon a single object, will be unattainable.'[4]

Still in his *Introductory Lectures* Freud stated that 'at puberty, when the sexual instinct first makes its demands in full strength, the old familiar incestuous objects are taken up again and freshly

[1] ibid., p. 177.
[2] (1925j) 'Some Psychological Consequences of the Anatomical Distinction between the Sexes', S.E., Vol. 19, p. 257.
[3] (1905d) *Three Essays on the Theory of Sexuality*, S.E., Vol. 7, p. 177.
[4] ibid., p. 200.

cathected with libido. The infantile object-choice was only a feeble one, but it was a prelude, pointing the direction for the object-choice at puberty. At this point, then, very intense emotional processes come into play, following the direction of the Oedipus complex or reacting against it, processes which, however, since their premises have become intolerable, must to a large extent remain apart from consciousness. From this time onwards, the human individual has to devote himself to the great task of detaching himself from his parents . . . it is remarkable how seldom they [these tasks] are dealt with in an ideal manner. . . . By neurotics, however, no solution at all is arrived at . . . '[1]

In the 1920s however, Freud developed the view definitively expressed in 'The Dissolution of The Oedipus Complex' that the crucial efforts in overcoming the Oedipus complex are those that coincide with the entry into latency; indeed, he implies that the formation of the superego is the precondition for the establishment of latency.[2]

In *The Ego and the Id* Freud drew on his work on melancholia where he had found that the loss of a love object is reacted to by a 'setting up of the object in the Ego' with a concomitant 'abandonment of sexual aims, a desexualization, a kind of sublimation', to show how the superego arises in consequence of the renunciation of the oedipal sexual objects, by means of the same identificatory mechanisms. '*The broad general outcome of the sexual phase dominated by the Oedipus complex may, therefore, be taken to be the forming of a precipitate in the ego, consisting of these two identifications in some way united with each other. This modification . . . confronts the other contents of the ego as an ego ideal or superego.*'[3]

At this time Freud seemed to view the need to abandon and repress the Oedipus complex as primarily due to the hereditarily determined onset of latency: 'the origin of the superego . . . is the outcome of two . . . factors . . . one of a biological and the other of a historical nature: . . . the lengthy duration in man of his childhood helplessnes and dependence, and the fact of his Oedipus complex, the repression of which we have shown to be connected with the interruption of libidinal development . . . and so with the diphasic onset of man's sexual life.'[4]

[1] (1916–17) *Introductory Lectures on Psycho-Analysis*, S.E., Vol. 16, p. 336 f.
[2] (1924d) 'The Dissolution of the Oedipus Complex', S.E., Vol. 19, p. 179.
[3] (1923b) *The Ego and the Id*, S.E., Vol. 19, p. 34.
[4] ibid., p. 35.

The recognition of the phallic phase in 'The Infantile Genital Organization' contributed the understanding that '*the significance of the castration complex can only be rightly appreciated if its origin in the phase of phallic primacy is taken into account*'.[1]

This led to the final formulation that 'what brings about the destruction of the child's phallic genital organization is this threat of castration',[2] that '*in boys the Oedipus complex is destroyed by the castration complex . . .*'[3]

In 1926, in *The Question of Lay Analysis*, Freud made explicit the corollary that the revival of the Oedipus complex in puberty is, though common not an ideal phenomenon: 'With the end of the early sexual period it [the Oedipus complex] should normally be given up, should radically disintegrate and become transformed; . . . But as a rule this is not effected radically enough, in which case puberty brings about a revival of the complex, which may have serious consequences.'[4]

III. *Causes of the Passing of the Oedipus Complex*
In 'The Dissolution of the Oedipus Complex', Freud discussed two views as to 'what it is that brings about its destruction'. One view is that it is the threat of castration and the experience of painful disappointments. 'In this way the Oedipus complex would go to its destruction from its lack of success, from the effects of its internal impossibility'.[5]

The other view stresses the maturational aspect: 'Another view is that the Oedipus complex must collapse because the time has come for its disintegration, just as the milk-teeth fall out when the permanent ones begin to grow. Although the majority of human beings go through the Oedipus complex as an individual experience, it is nevertheless a phenomenon which is determined and laid down by heredity and which is bound to pass away according to programme when the next preordained phase of development sets in.'[6]

[1] (1923e) 'The Infantile Genital Organization of the Libido', S.E., Vol. 19, p. 144.
[2] (1924d) 'The Dissolution of the Oedipus Complex' S.E., Vol. 19, p. 175.
[3] (1925j) 'Some Psychological Consequences of the Anatomical Distinction between the Sexes', S.E., Vol. 19, p. 256.
[4] (1926e) *The Question of Lay Analysis*, S.E., Vol. 20, p. 213.
[5] (1924d) 'The Dissolution of the Oedipus Complex', S.E., Vol. 19, p. 173.
[6] ibid., 173.

'The justice of both these views cannot be disputed. Moreover, they are compatible. There is room for the ontogenetic view side by side with the more far-reaching phylogenetic one. . . . Nevertheless, it remains of interest to follow out how this innate programme is carried out and in what way accidental noxae exploit his [the individual's] disposition'.[1]

In this paper, Freud spelled out how the 'termination' of the Oedipus complex 'takes place in a typical manner and in conjunction with events that are of regular recurrence'.[2]

' . . . what brings about the destruction of the child's phallic genital organization is this threat of castration.' The notion of the threat of castration may be seen as summarizing all the disapproval and frustration of the oedipal impulses, especially as manifested in masturbation, emanating from the parental figures, which as we see clinically, is elaborated by the child, via the mechanism of projection, into the threat of castration. Freud felt that typically the castration threat was 'more or less plainly' made, usually by the mother figure, as a punishment for masturbation. This threat was then reinforced by the boy's observation of sexual differences; he realizes that both positive and negative oedipal impulses face him with this threat. 'If the satisfaction of love in the field of the Oedipus complex is to cost the child his penis, a conflict is bound to arise between his narcissistic interest in that part of his body and the libidinal cathexis of his parental objects. In this conflict the first of these forces normally triumphs: the child's ego turns away from the Oedipus complex.'[3] 'The whole process [of turning away from the Oedipus complex] has, on the one hand, preserved the genital organ—has averted the danger of its loss—and, on the other, has paralysed it—has removed its function. This process ushers in the latency period. . . .'[4]

We may also mention here that Freud always had a strong sense of the teleological significance of the overcoming of the Oedipus complex.

' . . . the emphasis laid upon the relation of children to their parents is an expression of the biological facts that the young of the human race pass through a long period of dependence and are slow in reaching maturity, as well as that their capacity for love undergoes a complicated course of development. Consequently,

[1] ibid., p. 174.   [2] ibid., p. 174.
[3] ibid., p. 175 f.   [4] ibid., p. 177.

the overcoming of the Oedipus complex coincides with the most efficient way of mastering the archaic, animal heritage of humanity. It is true that that heritage comprises all the forces that are required for the subsequent cultural development of the individual, but they must first be sorted out and worked over. This archaic heirloom is not fit to be used for the purposes of civilized social life in the form in which it is inherited by the individual.'[1]

IV. *Metapsychological Implications of the Dissolution of the Oedipus Complex*

The metapsychological implications of the dissolution of the Oedipus complex are most fully spelled out by Freud in chapter III of *The Ego and the Id*, and resummarized in the quotation given in our definition. In *The Ego and the Id* discussion, Freud asks the question why, when the boy abandons his oedipal erotic cathexis of the mother, it is replaced, apparently, by identifications with the father, rather than with the primary lost love object, the mother. He answers this question in terms of bisexuality and of the fourfold aspect of the full Oedipus complex, i.e., the existence of both a positive and negative Oedipus complex, with both affectionate and hostile impulses towards each parents.

' . . . in both sexes the relative strength of the masculine and feminine sexual dispositions is what determines whether the outcome of the Oedipus situation shall be an identification with the father or with the mother.'[2] 'At the dissolution of the Oedipus complex the four trends of which it consists will group themselves in such a way as to produce a father-identification and a mother-identification. The father-identification will preserve the object-relation to the mother which belonged to the positive complex and will at the same time replace the object-relation to the father which belonged to the inverted complex: and the same will be true, *mutatis mutandis*, of the mother-identification. The relative intensity of the two identifications in any individual will reflect the preponderance in him of one or other of the two sexual dispositions.'[3]

With the 'abandonment of sexual aims' and the transformation of

---

[1] (1919g) Preface to Reik's *Ritual: Psycho-Analytic Studies*, S.E., Vol. 17, p. 261 f.

[2] (1923b) *The Ego and the Id*, S.E., Vol. 19, p. 33.

[3] ibid., p. 34.

object cathexes into identifications, the libido undergoes qualitative changes to which Freud gives special attention in this context. 'The transformation of object-libido into narcissistic libido which thus takes place obviously implies an abandonment of sexual aims, a desexualization—a kind of sublimation, therefore.'[1]

He further suggests that such sublimation always results in a defusion of the libidinal and aggressive components of the object cathexes; in the process of the dissolution of the Oedipus complex, the liberated aggressive component serves to form the aggressive element of the superego.

'The superego arises, as we know, from an identification with the father taken as a model. Every such identification is in the nature of a desexualization or even of a sublimation. It now seems as though when a transformation of this kind takes place, an instinctual defusion occurs at the same time.'[2]

V. *The Dissolution of the Oedipus Complex in the Female* (See Concept: The Oedipus Complex in Girls)
The work done in the 1920s which showed that in girls the oedipal phase follows a different course of development from that in boys, together with Freud's recognition that in boys it was castration anxiety which motivated the abandonment of the oedipal ties, brought about the rethinking of Freud's prior assumption that the overcoming of the Oedipus complex is carried out in a similar manner in girls and in boys.

In 'The Dissolution of the Oedipus Complex', Freud already envisaged this problem: 'The fear of castration being thus excluded in the little girl, a powerful motive also drops out for the setting-up of a super-ego and for the breaking-off of the infantile genital organization. In her, far more than in the boy, these changes seem to be the result of upbringing and of intimidation from outside which threatens her with a loss of love . . . One has an impression that the Oedipus complex is then gradually given up because this wish (to have a child from the father) is never fulfilled.'[3]

The study of the oedipal phase in girls brought into prominence the prolonged negative-oedipal relationship to the mother which in girls precedes the positive oedipus complex, and showed that it is mainly the girl's castration complex which leads her to turn

[1] ibid., p. 30.   [2] ibid., p. 54.
[3] (1924d) 'The Dissolution of the Oedipus Complex', S.E., Vol. 19, p. 1/8 f.

from the mother to the father. In 'Some Psychological Con-sequence of the Anatomical Distinction Between the Sexes' Freud drew the conclusion that a dissolution of the Oedipus complex in the sense that it occurs in boys is not possible in female development. *'Whereas in boys the Oedipus complex is destroyed by the castration complex, in girls it is made possible and led up by the castration complex.'*[1] 'In girls the motive for the demolition of the Oedipus complex is lacking. . . . the Oedipus complex . . . may be slowly abandoned or dealt with by repression, or its effects may persist far into women's normal mental life.'[2] He suggests as a consequence that women's 'superego is never so inexorable, so impersonal, so independent of its emotional origins as we require it to be in men'.[3]

This view is adumbrated in the 1931 paper 'Female Sexuality'. The Oedipus complex 'is all too often not surmounted by the female at all. For this reason, too, the cultural consequences of its break-up are smaller and of less importance in her . . . probably . . . it is the difference in the reciprocal relation between the Oedipus and the castration complex which gives its special stamp to the character of females as social beings'.[4]

And in the chapter on female sexuality in the *New Introductory Lectures*, Freud gave as his final formulation, 'Girls remain in it for an indeterminate length of time; they demolish it late and, even so, incompletely'.[5]

'For girls the Oedipus situation is the outcome of a long and difficult development; it is a kind of preliminary solution, a position of rest which is not soon abandoned, especially as the beginning of the latency period is not far distant.'[6]

---

[1] (1925j) 'Some Psychological Consequences of the Anatomical Distinction between the Sexes', S.E., Vol. 19, p. 256.
[2] ibid., p. 257.
[3] ibid., p. 257.
[4] (1931b) 'Female Sexuality', S.E., Vol. 21, p. 230.
[5] (1933a) *New Introductory Lectures on Psycho-Analysis*, S.E., Vol. 22, p. 129.
[6] ibid., p. 129.

LATENCY

SEE CONCEPT: *The Oedipus Complex*

Introduction

'Latency', a term originally used by Fliess and later adopted by Freud,[1] refers to a period of diminished sexual activity in the physical development of the individual.

It begins at the end of the fifth year (up to 1924 Freud had put the beginning of latency at the end of the fourth year) and continues to the beginning of puberty around the eleventh year.[2]

The beginning of this period is 'characterized by the dissolution of the Oedipus complex, the creation or consolidation of the superego and the erection of ethical and aesthetic barriers in the ego'.[3] After the Oedipal phase the activities of the infantile sexual impulses do not cease, but rather are 'overtaken by a progressive process of suppression'.[4] Moreover, 'their energy is diverted, wholly or in great part, from their sexual use and directed to other ends'.[5] Furthermore, a relative cessation in the growth of the external genitalia is noticeable.[6] 'The chief task during the latency period seems to be the fending-off of the temptation to masturbate.'[7] However, it would seem that the child has a very active phantasy life. 'It is a puzzling fact that boys take such an extraordinarily intense interest in things connected with railways, and, at an age at which the production of phantasies is most active (shortly before puberty), use those things as the nucleus of a symbolism that is peculiarly sexual.'[8]

When explaining how much goes on in children of four or five years and how active their minds are, Freud also stated: 'I have an impression that with the onset of the latency period they

---

[1] (1905d) *Three Essays on the Theory of Sexuality*, S.E., Vol. 7, p. 178, n.1.
[2] (1908b) 'Character and Anal Erotism', S.E., Vol. 9, p. 171 and n.1.
[3] (1926d) *Inhibitions, Symptoms and Anxiety*, S.E., Vol. 20, p. 114.
[4] (1905d) *Three Essays on the Theory of Sexuality*, S.E., Vol. 7, p. 176.
[5] ibid., p. 178.
[6] ibid., p. 208.
[7] (1926d) *Inhibitions, Symptoms and Anxiety*, S.E., Vol. 20, p. 116.
[8] (1905d) *Three Essays on the Theory of Sexuality*, S.E., Vol. 7, p. 202.

83

become mentally inhibited as well, stupider. From that time on, too, many children lose their physical charm.'[1]

Explanations for the Period of Latency

Recognizing the absence of a latency period in the development of animals and contrasting it with that found in humans, Freud offered two main explanations: (1) a biological and ontogenetic one, and (2) a phylogenetic one. 'This diphasic development of the sexual function—in two stages, interrupted by the latency period— appears to be a biological peculiarity of the human species and to contain the determining factor for the origin of neuroses.'[2] Latency is the outgrowth of the resolved Oedipus complex: 'In this way the Oedipus complex would go to its destruction from its lack of success, from the effects of its internal impossibility.

'Another view is that the Oedipus complex must collapse because the time has come for its disintegration, just as the milk-teeth fall out when the permanent ones begin to grow. Although the majority of human beings go through the Oedipus complex as an individual experience, it is nevertheless a phenomenon which is determined and laid down by heredity and which is bound to pass away according to programme when the next preordained phase of development sets in. This being so, it is of no great importance what the occasions are which allow this to happen, or, indeed, whether any such occasions can be discovered at all.

'The justice of both these views cannot be disputed. Moreover, they are compatible. There is room for the ontogenetic view side by side with the more far-reaching phylogenetic one'.[3]

Freud also asserted that education might play a part in the consolidation of the latency period. 'One gets an impression from civilized children that the construction of these dams is a product of education, and no doubt education has much to do with it. But in reality this development is organically determined and fixed by heredity, and it can occasionally occur without any help at all from education. Education will not be trespassing beyond its appropriate domain if it limits itself to following the lines which have already been laid down organically and to impressing them somewhat more clearly and deeply.'[4] This led him, in 1935, to add

[1] (1926e) *The Question of Lay Analysis*, S.E., Vol. 20, p. 215.
[2] (1923a) 'Two Encyclopaedia Articles', S.E., Vol. 18, p. 246.
[3] (1924d) 'The Dissolution of the Oedipus Complex', S.E., Vol. 19, p. 173 f.
[4] (1905d) *Three Essays on the Theory of Sexuality*, S.E., Vol. 7, p. 177 f.

the note: 'The period of latency is a physiological phenomenon. It can, however, only give rise to a complete interruption of sexual life in cultural organizations which have made the suppression of infantile sexuality a part of their system. This is not the case with the majority of primitive peoples.'[1] Freud also pointed out, however, that external influences may not only consolidate the latency period but that seductions during it may lead to its interruption. Thus he states in *The Three Essays*: 'Experience further showed that the external influences of seduction are capable of provoking interruptions of the latency period or even its cessation, and that in this connection the sexual instinct of children proves in fact to be polymorphously perverse; it seems, moreover, that any such premature sexual activity diminishes a child's educability.'[2] With reference to this quotation it should be borne in mind, however, that at the time it was written Freud had not as yet made a clear distinction between actual seduction during childhood and fantasies of seduction based on a wish to have been seduced.

Although aware of the gaps in knowledge about this period Freud first described it in his *Three Essays on the Theory of Sexuality* in 1905 and except for the additional note in 1935 (mentioned above) did not change or elaborate on his original thesis. 'We must not deceive ourselves as to the hypothetical nature and insufficient clarity of our knowledge concerning the processes of the infantile period of latency or deferment; but we shall be on firmer ground in pointing out that such an application of infantile sexuality represents an educational ideal from which individual development usually diverges at some point and often to a considerable degree.'[3] Freud probably had such deviations from the ideal in mind when he wrote in a letter to Pfister in 1926: 'In regard to . . . the latency period, . . . the setting aside of sexuality is often only partial, with the result that a certain amount of activity is maintained. That is very frequent, and there are also plenty of cases with which one would never have hit on the idea of a latency period at all'.[4]

[1] [1935] (1925d [1924]) *An Autobiographical Study*, S.E., Vol. 20, p. 37, n. 1.

[2] (1905d) *Three Essays on the Theory of Sexuality*, S.E., Vol. 7, p. 234.

[3] ibid., p. 179.

[4] [1926] Pfister, O., *Psycho-analysis and Faith*, Hogarth Press, London, 1963, p. 105.

Normal Outcome of Latency

Repression of the infantile sexual wishes is the most outstanding feature of the latency period: 'None of these incestuous loves can avoid the fate of repression. . . . Most probably they pass away because their time is over, because the children have entered upon a new phase of development in which they are compelled to re-capitulate from the history of mankind the repression of an in-cestuous object-choice, just as at an earlier stage they were obliged to effect an object-choice of that very sort. In the new phase no mental product of the incestuous love-impulses that is present unconsciously is taken over by consciousness; and anything that has already come into consciousness is expelled from it. At the same time as this process of repression takes place, a sense of guilt appears. This is also of unknown origin, but there is no doubt whatever that it is connected with the incestuous wishes, and that it is justified by the persistence of those wishes in the unconscious.'[1]

With the passing of the Oedipal complex the libidinal impulses are repressed and 'are in part desexualized and sublimated (a thing which probably happens with every transformation into an identi-fication) and in part inhibited in their aim and changed into impulses of affection.'[2] Thus we see the early beginnings of social order, religion and morality.[3] Myths, works of imaginative writing and art are also considered sublimations and substitute satisfactions for the repressed wishes of childhood.[4]

Furthermore, reaction formations appear: 'the sexual impulses which have shown liveliness are overcome by repression, and a *period of latency* follows, which lasts until puberty and during which the *reaction formations* of morality, shame, and disgust are built up'.[5]

It is also during this period that the division between the ego and the superego becomes consolidated. 'The authority of the father or the parents is introjected into the ego, and there it forms the nucleus of the superego, which takes over the severity of the father.'[6]

Moreover, the character of the person, along with his habitual

[1] (1919e) 'A Child is Being Beaten', S.E., Vol. 17, p. 188.
[2] (1924d) 'The Dissolution of the Oedipus Complex', S.E., Vol. 19, p. 177.
[3] (1923b) *The Ego and the Id*, S.E., Vol. 19, p. 37.
[4] (1924f) 'A Short Account of Psycho-Analysis', S.E., Vol. 19, p. 207 f.
[5] (1925d [1924]) *An Autobiographical Study*, S.E. Vol., 20, p. 37.
[6] (1924d) 'The Dissolution of the Oedipus Complex', S.E., Vol. 19, p. 176 f.

manner of handling internal and external demands, becomes consolidated during this time. 'I have no doubt that the chronological and causal relations described . . . between the Oedipus complex, sexual intimidation (the threat of castration), the formation of the superego and the beginning of the latency period are of a typical kind; but I do not wish to assert that this type is the only possible one. Variations in the chronological order and in the linking-up of these events are bound to have a very important bearing on the development of the individual'.[1]

Freud concluded, however, that absolute latency is a myth. 'From time to time a fragmentary manifestation of sexuality which has evaded sublimation may break through; or some sexual activity may persist through the whole duration of the latency period until the sexual instinct emerges with greater intensity at puberty.'[2]

Clinical Application

Symptoms of certain clinical conditions sometimes start during latency. This is particularly true in the case of obsessional neuroses: 'obsessional neurosis usually shows its first symptoms in the second period of childhood (between the ages of six and eight)'.[3]

'Ceremonial actions appear extremely often in the latency period, but only a very small percentage of them develop later into a full obsessional neurosis.'[4]

[1] ibid., p. 179.
[2] (1905d) *Three Essays on the Theory of Sexuality*, S.E., Vol. 7, p. 179.
[3] (1913i) 'The Predisposition to Obsessional Neurosis', S.E., Vol. 12, p. 318.
[4] (1926d) *Inhibitions, Symptoms and Anxiety*, S.E., Vol. 20, p. 147.

GENITAL EROTISM

Genital erotism is defined as comprising those drives characteristic of the genital phase of development. 'We have reserved the name of *genital* phase for the definitive sexual organization which is established after puberty and in which the female genital organ for the first time meets with the recognition which the male one acquired long before.'[1] In the *Outline* Freud referred to the genital phase as the fourth libidinal phase, i.e. succeeding the oral, anal, and phallic phases. He states that the complete organization of the sexual function 'is only achieved at puberty, in a fourth, genital phase. A state of things is then established in which (1) some earlier libidinal cathexes are retained, (2) others are taken into the sexual function as preparatory, auxiliary acts, the satisfaction of which produces what is known as fore-pleasure, and (3) other urges are excluded from the organization, and are either suppressed altogether (repressed) or are employed in the ego in another way, forming character-traits or undergoing sublimation with a displacement of their aims'.[2] These formulations represent Freud's final statements with regard to the genital phase. However, considerable changes in his views on libidinal development had preceded them. With regard to the genital phase there are three aspects in particular which are of relevance as far as the development of Freud's views is concerned, all stated in his 'Five Lectures':

1. The concept that 'the whole sexual life [in puberty] enters the service of reproduction, and the satisfaction of the separate instincts retains its importance only as preparing for and encouraging the sexual act proper'[3] is elaborated in terms of the physical changes of puberty. Essentially this aspect of Freud's concept of genitality was not changed.

2. In the 'Five Lectures' Freud views childhood as essentially autoerotic and states that object choice takes place only after puberty. With the discovery of the pre-genital phases this view was much modified and will be described below.

[1] (1933a) *New Introductory Lectures on Psycho-Analysis*, S.E., Vol. 22, p. 99.
[2] (1940a [1938]) *An Outline of Psycho-Analysis*, S.E., Vol. 23, p. 155.
[3] (1910a [1909]) 'Five Lectures on Psycho-Analysis,' S.E., Vol. 11, p. 45.

88

3. With the discovery of the phallic phase of development before latency Freud introduced a phase sometimes described as a first phase of genitality. As will be shown, it is in a sense, a genital phase during which, however, only the male genital is required.

The importance of this concept in psychoanalytic thinking was indicated in the following quotation in which it is referred to in contrast to the pre-genital phases of childhood which had been seen as autoerotic. 'Psycho-analysis stands or falls with the recognition of the sexual component instincts, of the erotogenic zones and of the extension thus made possible of the concept of a "sexual function" in contrast to the narrower "genital function".'[1]

The following quotation elaborates on the above and shows how Freud regarded the degree and type of failure to reach genital dominance as an indication for the assessment of pathology.

'This widespread and copious but dissociated sexual life of children, in which each separate instinct pursues its own acquisition of pleasure independently of all the rest, is now brought together and organized in two main directions, so that by the end of puberty the individual's final sexual character is as a rule completely formed. On the one hand, the separate instincts become subordinated to the dominance of the genital zone, so that the whole sexual life enters the service of reproduction, and the satisfaction of the separate instincts retains its importance only as preparing for and encouraging the sexual act proper. On the other hand, object-choice pushes autoerotism into the background, so that in the subject's erotic life all the components of the sexual instinct now seek satisfaction in relation to the person who is loved. Not all of the original sexual components, however, are admitted to take part in this final establishment of sexuality. Even before puberty extremely energetic repressions of certain instincts have been effected under the influence of education, and mental forces such as shame, disgust and morality have been set up, which, like watchmen, maintain these repressions. So that when at puberty the high tide of sexual demands is reached, it is met by these mental reactive or resistant structures like dams, which direct its flow into what are called normal channels and make it impossible for it to reactivate the instincts that have undergone repression.

' . . . every developmental process carries with it the seed of a pathological disposition, in so far as that process may be inhibited,

[1] (1913i) 'The Predisposition to Obsessional Neurosis', S.E., Vol. 12, p. 323.

delayed, or may run its course incompletely . . . the sexual function . . . does not occur smoothly in every individual. . . . It may
happen that not all the component instincts submit to the dominance of the genital zone.' [Freud then describes how perversion
or neurosis may result.][1]

In a 1915-addition to the *Three Essays* Freud wrote:

'The final outcome of sexual development lies in what is known
as the normal sexual life of the adult, in which the pursuit of
pleasure comes under the sway of the reproductive function and
in which the component instincts, under the primacy of a single
erotogenic zone, form a firm organization directed towards a sexual
aim attached to some extraneous sexual object.'[2]

1. The Physical Changes of Puberty

Freud describes the way in which the reproductive function
develops during puberty from the physical and psychological
point of view, these being interrelated. Thus a highly complicated
apparatus [which] has been made ready and awaits the moment of
being put into operation, produces "sexual excitement" which
shows itself by two sorts of indication, mental and somatic.[3]

Later he wrote that during latency 'the genital zones already
behave in much the same way as in maturity; they become the seat
of sensations of excitation and of preparatory changes whenever
any pleasure is felt from the satisfaction of other erotogenic zones,
though this result is still without a purpose—that is to say, contributes nothing to a continuation of the sexual process . . . in childhood, therefore, alongside of the pleasure of satisfaction there is
. . . sexual tension, although it is less constant and less in quantity'.[4]

2. The Timing of Object Choice

The early formulations of childhood as being essentially autoerotic
in nature were made before the discovery of the pregenital phases
of development. Freud later postulated that the first signs (or
forerunners) of object love (i.e. where the object is loved as a
person in its own right) can be observed in the anal phase. It also
preceded the discovery of the phallic phase in which a different
type of object choice takes place.

---

[1] (1910a[1909]) 'Five Lectures on Psycho-Analysis', S.E., Vol. 11, p. 44 f.
[2] [1915] (1905d) *Three Essays on the Theory of Sexuality*, S.E., Vol. 7, p. 197.
[3] ibid., p. 208.   [4] ibid., p. 212 f.

In sections of the *Three Essays* which were added in 1915 these earlier views are modified as follows:

'In order to complete our picture of infantile sexual life, we must also suppose that the choice of an object, such as we have shown to be characteristic of the pubertal phase of development, has already frequently or habitually been effected during the years of childhood: that is to say, the whole of the sexual currents have become directed towards a single person in relation to whom they seek to achieve their aims. This then is the closest approximation possible in childhood to the final form taken by sexual life after puberty.'[1]

In another addition Freud refers to the 'diphasic' quality of object choice: 'It may be regarded as typical of the choice of an object that the process is diphasic, that is, that it occurs in two waves. The first of these begins between the ages of two and five, and is brought to a halt or to a retreat by the latency period; it is characterized by the infantile nature of the sexual aims. The second wave sets in with puberty and determines the final outcome of sexual life.'[2]

The following paragraph was added in 1920: 'We were then obliged to recognize, as one of our most surprising findings, that this early efflorescence of infantile sexual life (between the ages of two and five) already gives rise to the choice of an object, with all the wealth of mental activities which such a process involves.'[3]

3. *The Discovery of the Phallic Phase*

In 1924 the following footnote was added: 'At a later date (1923) I myself modified this account by inserting a third phase in the development of childhood, subsequent to the two pregenital organizations. This phase, which already deserves to be described as genital, presents a sexual object and some degree of convergence of the sexual impulses upon that object; but it is differentiated from the final organization of sexual maturity in one essential respect. For it knows only one kind of genital: the male one. For that reason I have named it the "phallic" stage of organization. (Freud 1923). According to Abraham (1924), it has a biological prototype in the embryo's undifferentiated genital disposition, which is the same for both sexes.'[4]

Later he wrote of the phallic phase of infantile sexuality

---

[1] [1915] ibid., p. 199. [2] [1915] ibid., p. 200.
[3] [1920] ibid., p. 234. [4] [1924] ibid., p. 199 f.

' . . . "this genital is the male one only, or, more correctly, the penis; the female genital has remained undiscovered . . . contemporaneous with the Oedipus complex, [the phallic phase] does not develop further to the definitive genital organization, but is submerged, and is succeeded by the latency period. Its termination, however, takes place in a typical manner and in conjunction with events that are of regular recurrence'. There follows an account of the castration threat, which plays its part in the destruction of phallic sexual organization.[1]

Similarly Freud states in another paper:

'Before this [puberty], and while the child is at the highest point of its infantile sexual development, a genital organization of a sort is established; but only the male genitals play a part in it, and the female ones remain undiscovered. (I have described this as the period of *phallic* primacy.) At this stage the contrast between the sexes is not stated in terms of 'male' or 'female' but of "possessing a penis" or "castrated".'[2]

The Discovery of the Female Organ

'It is not unimportant to bear in mind what transformations are undergone, during the sexual development of childhood, by the polarity of sex with which we are familiar. A first antithesis is introduced with the choice of object, which, of course, presupposes a subject and an object. At the stage of the pregenital sadistic-anal organization, there is as yet no question of male and female; the antithesis between *active* and *passive* is the dominant one. At the following stage of infantile genital organization, which we now know about, *maleness* exists, but not femaleness. The antithesis here is between having a *male* genital and being *castrated*. It is not until development has reached its completion at puberty that the sexual polarity coincides with *male* and *female*. Maleness combines [the factors of] subject, activity and possession of the penis; femaleness takes over [those of] object and passivity. The vagina is now valued as a place of shelter for the penis; it enters into the heritage of the womb.'[3]

One of the implicit assumptions is that it is only in the genital phase that object choice can be made on the basis of sexual

[1] (1924d) 'The Dissolution of the Oedipus Complex', S.E., Vol. 19, p. 174.
[2] (1925d) *An Autobiographical Study*, S.E., Vol. 20, p. 37.
[3] (1923e) 'The Infantile Genital Organization', S.E., Vol. 19, p. 145.

difference rather than that of competition, exhibitionism, etc., as in the phallic phase.

The other assumption of a genital phase is that essentially it represents an ultimate—and in many ways similar—step in development for both sexes although Freud considers that 'the development of a little girl into a normal woman is more difficult'[1] because of the complicated changes both with regard to the erotogenic zone, i.e. from clitoris to vagina, and with regard to object-choice, i.e. from the female to the male object.[2] Essentially there are equal dangers of not reaching this phase for both sexes. In writing of the difficulty for the girl in overcoming her castration complex, Freud wrote: 'This means, therefore, that as a result of the discovery of women's lack of a penis they are debased in value for girls just as they are for boys and later perhaps for men.'[3]

As to the necessary change in girls with regard to their erotogenic zone, Freud states:

'The sexuality of female children is, as we know, dominated and directed by a masculine organ (the clitoris) and often behaves like the sexuality of boys. This masculine sexuality has to be got rid of by a last wave of development at puberty, and the vagina, an organ derived from the cloaca, has to be raised into the dominant erotogenic zone.'[4]

The Fusion of Drives
The fusion of sexual and aggressive instincts is an essential characteristic of the genital phase of development.

'At the higher stage of the pregenital sadistic-anal organization, the striving for the object appears in the form of an urge for mastery, to which injury or annihilation of the object is a matter of indifference. Love in this form and at this preliminary stage is hardly to be distinguished from hate in its attitude toward the object. Not until the genital organization is established does love become the opposite of hate.

' . . . When the ego-instincts dominate the sexual function, as

[1] (1933a) *New Introductory Lectures on Psycho-Analysis*, S.E., Vol. 22, p. 117.
[2] (1925j) 'Some Psychological Consequences of the Anatomical Distinction between the Sexes', S.E., Vol. 19. p. 251.
[3] (1933a) *New Introductory Lectures on Psycho-Analysis*, S.E., Vol. 22, p. 127.
[4] (1913i) 'The Disposition to Obsessional Neurosis', S.E., Vol. 12, p. 325 f.

is the case at the stage of the sadistic-anal organization, they impart the qualities of hate to the instinctual aim as well.'[1]

Elsewhere Freud states:

'Erotogenic masochism accompanies the libido through all its developmental phases and derives from them its changing psychical coatings. The fear of being eaten up by the totem animal (the father) originates from the primitive oral organization; the wish to be beaten by the father comes from the sadistic-anal phase which follows it; castration, although it is later disavowed, enters into the content of masochistic fantasies as a precipitate of the phallic stage or organization; and from the final genital organization there arise, of course, the situations of being copulated with and of giving birth which are characteristic of femaleness.'[2]

The sadistic instinct 'separates off, and finally, at the stage of genital primacy, it takes on, for the purposes of reproduction, the function of overpowering the sexual object to the extent necessary for carrying out the sexual act'.[3]

The Genital Phase in Relation to Personality, Character Development and Social Aims

In the following quotation the relation between the co-ordination of all sexual instincts under the primacy of the genital organization and personality integration is pointed out.

Freud showed that children can keep ambivalent feelings to the same person for long periods of time; when conflict emerges, one part is displaced to another, substitute object: 'In the process of a child's development into a mature adult there is a more and more extensive integration of his personality, a co-ordination of the separate instinctual impulses and purposive trends which have grown up in him independently of one another. The analogous process in the domain of sexual life has long been known to us as the co-ordination of all the sexual instincts into a definitive genital organization.'[4]

'A normal sexual life is only assured by an exact convergence of the affectionate current and the sensual current both being directed towards the sexual object and sexual aim. . . . It is like the com-

[1] (1915c) 'Instincts and their Vicissitudes', S.E., Vol. 14, p. 138 f.
[2] (1924c) 'The Economic Problem of Masochism', S.E., Vol. 19, p. 164 f.
[3] (1920g) *Beyond the Pleasure Principle*, S.E., Vol. 18, p. 54.
[4] (1921c) *Group Psychology and the Analysis of the Ego*, S.E., Vol. 18, p. 79 f. n.

pletion of a tunnel which has been driven through a hill from both directions.

'The new sexual aim in men consists in the discharge of the sexual products. The earlier one, the attainment of pleasure, is by no means alien to it; on the contrary, the highest degree of pleasure is attached to this final act of the sexual process. The sexual instinct is now subordinated to the reproductive function; it becomes, so to say, altruistic. If this transformation is to succeed, the original dispositions and all the other characteristics of the instincts must be taken into account in the process.'[1]

Sublimation

Many of Freud's formulations seem to imply that sublimations are more easily and effectively achieved by individuals with a genital (i.e., social) character, whereas such sublimations are more difficult to achieve and maintain for people whose character structure is based on pre-genital fixations, which tend to reveal much more selfish aims. Freud alludes to this in the following quotation from the *Introductory Lectures*: 'There are in general very many ways of tolerating deprivation of libidinal satisfaction without falling ill as a result. In the first place, we know people who are able to put up with a deprivation of this kind without being injured: they are not happy, they suffer from longing, but they do not fall ill. Next, we must bear in mind that the sexual instinctual impulses in particular are extraordinarily *plastic*, if I may so express it. One of them can take the place of another, one of them can take over another's intensity; if the satisfaction of one of them is frustrated by reality, the satisfaction of another can afford complete compensation. They are related to one another like a network of inter-communicating channels filled with a liquid; and this is so in spite of their being subject to the primacy of the genitals—a state of affairs that is not at all easily combined in a single picture. Further, the component instincts of sexuality, as well as the sexual current which is compounded from them, exhibit a large capacity for changing their object, for taking another in its place—and one, therefore, that is more easily attainable. This displaceability and readiness to accept a substitute must operate powerfully against the pathogenic effect of a frustration. Among these protective processes against falling ill owing to deprivation there is one which has

[1] (1905d) *Three Essays on the Theory of Sexuality*, S.E., Vol. 7, p. 207.

gained special cultural significance. It consists in the sexual trend
abandoning its aim of obtaining a component or a reproductive
pleasure and taking on another which is related genetically to the
abandoned one but is itself no longer sexual and must be described
as social. We call this process 'sublimation', in accordance with the
general estimate that places social aims higher than the sexual ones,
which are at bottom self-interested.'[1]

[1] (1916–17) *Introductory Lectures on Psycho-Analysis*, S.E., Vol. 16, p. 345.

LIBIDINAL DEVELOPMENT AT PUBERTY

SEE CONCEPTS: *Phallic Erotism, Genital Erotism, Oedipus Complex, Dissolution of Oedipus Complex*

Although Freud referred to the period of puberty throughout his writings, the basis of the examination of changes occurring at this period were laid down in *Three Essays on Sexuality*.[1] Important additions discussing the changes at puberty were added to this essay, especially after Freud had written his paper 'On Narcissism' (1914).[2]

I. *Definition*

Puberty is that period of life when the physical primacy of the genital zone is attained. (In present day usage, a person may have reached puberty in the physical sense, and still not be properly speaking an adolescent, that is, may not have taken the psychological steps that characterize adolescence.)

'The complete organization [which subordinates the other urges to the primacy of the genitals and signifies the start of a coordination of the general urge towards pleasure into the sexual function] is only achieved at puberty, in a fourth, genital phase. A state of things is then established in which (1) some earlier libidinal cathexes are retained, (2) others are taken into the sexual function as preparatory, auxiliary acts, the satisfaction of which produces what is known as fore-pleasure, and (3) other urges are excluded from the organization, and are either suppressed altogether (repressed) or are employed in the ego in another way, forming character-traits or undergoing sublimation with a displacement of their aims.'[3]

An essential characteristic of the processes taking place during puberty is that the 'instinctual elements attaching to the repressed

---

[1] (1905d) *Three Essays on the Theory of Sexuality*, S.E., Vol. 7.
[2] (1914c) 'On Narcissism: an Introduction', S.E., Vol. 14.
[3] (1940a [1938]) *An Outline of Psycho-Analysis*, S.E., Vol. 23, p. 155.

receive a special reinforcement'.[1] Freud elsewhere points out that 'twice in the course of individual development certain instincts are considerably reinforced: at puberty, and in women, at the meno-pause'.[2] Freud also considered that neurosis which began during the period of early childhood was usually interrupted by 'a period of apparently undisturbed development—a course of things which is supported or made possible by the intervention of the physio-logical period of latency. Not until later does the change take place with which the definitive neurosis becomes manifest as a belated effect of the trauma. This occurs either at the irruption of puberty or some while later. In the former case it happens because the instincts, intensified by physical maturation, are able now to take up the struggle again in which they were at first defeated by the defence'.[3] Freud saw homosexuality as likely to be established after puberty[4] and he considered that masturbation was a char-acteristic feature of puberty.[5]

II. *History of Concept*

Freud's first extensive description on the libidinal development at puberty were discussed in the *Three Essays*. In his later writings, he elaborated on this, with the emphasis in his writings changing from the major rearrangement taking place at puberty to the emphasis being on the crucial changes in psychosexual development and in object relationships taking place during the phallic-oedipal period, that is, some time from the age of three to five.

'With the arrival of puberty, changes set in which are destined to give infantile sexual life its final, normal shape. The sexual instinct has hitherto been derived from a number of separate instincts and erotogenic zones, which, independently of one another, have pursued a certain sort of pleasure as their sole sexual aim. Now, however, a new sexual aim appears, and all the component instincts combine to attain it, while the erotogenic

[1] (1939a) *Moses and Monotheism*, S.E., Vol. 23, p. 95.

[2] (1937c) 'Analysis Terminable and Interminable', S.E., Vol. 23, p. 226.

[3] (1939a) *Moses and Monotheism*, S.E., Vol. 23, p. 77, cf. (1909a) 'Some General Remarks on Hysterical Attacks', S.E., Vol. 9, p. 234, and (1926d) *Inhibitions, Symptoms and Anxiety*, S.E., Vol. 20, p. 116.

[4] (1922b) 'Some Neurotic Mechanisms in Jealousy, Paranoia and Homo-sexuality' S.E., Vol. 18, p. 230 f.

[5] (1905d) *Three Essays on the Theory of Sexuality*, S.E., Vol. 7, p. 189.

zones become subordinated to the primacy of the genital zone.'[1]

In *Three Essays*, Freud also showed the relation of the physical changes taking place at puberty to the physical relation to objects. 'The most striking of the processes at puberty has been picked upon as constituting its essence: the manifest growth of the external genitalia. (The latency period of childhood is, on the other hand, characterized by a relative cessation of their growth.) In the meantime the development of the internal genitalia has advanced far enough for them to be able to discharge the sexual products or, as the case may be, to bring about the formation of a new living organism. Thus a highly complicated apparatus has been made ready and awaits the moment of being put into operation.'[2] Later, in the same essay, under the sub-heading 'The Finding of an Object' Freud states, 'The processes at puberty thus establish the primacy of the genital zones; and, in a man, the penis, which has now become capable of erection, presses forward insistently towards the new sexual aim—penetration into a cavity in the body which excites his genital zone. Simultaneously on the physical side the process of finding an object, for which preparations have been made from earliest childhood, is completed.[3]

In his paper on 'The Infantile Genital Organization' (1923), in which he states the changes in his views since the *Three Essays*, he writes, 'Today I should no longer be satisfied with the statement that in the early period of childhood the primacy of the genitals has been effected only very incompletely or not at all. The approximation of the child's sexual life to that of the adult goes much further and is not limited solely to the coming into being of the choice of an object. Even if a proper combination of the component instincts under the primacy of the genitals is not effected, nevertheless, at the height of the course of development of infantile sexuality, interest in the genitals and in their activity acquires a dominating significance which falls little short of that reached in maturity. At the same time, the main characteristic of this "infantile genital organization" is its *difference* from the final genital organization of the adult. This consists in the fact that, for both sexes, only one genital, namely the male one, comes into

---

[1] (1905d) *Three Essays on the Theory of Sexuality*, S.E., Vol. 7, p. 207, cf. (1908d) ' "Civilized" Sexual Ethics and Modern Nervous Illness', S.E., Vol. 9, p. 133 f.

[2] ibid., p. 208.   [3] Ibid., p. 222.

THE LIBIDO THEORY

account. What is present, therefore, is not a primacy of the genitals, but a primacy of the *phallus*.'[1]

The physical capacity for discharge at puberty is the important distinction made by Freud between phallic erotism and genital erotism. He now also stresses the important difference in the further sexual development of men and women. 'The leading erotogenic zone in female children is located at the clitoris, and is thus homologous to the masculine genital zone of the glans penis. All my experience concerning masturbation in little girls has related to the clitoris and not to the regions of the external genitalia that are important in later sexual functioning. . . . If we are to understand how a little girl turns into a woman, we must follow the further vicissitudes of this excitability of the clitoris. Puberty, which brings about so great an accession of libido in boys, is marked in girls by a fresh wave of *repression*, in which it is precisely clitoridal sexuality that is affected. What is thus overtaken by repression is a piece of masculine sexuality. The intensification of the brake upon sexuality brought about by pubertal repression in woman serves as a stimulus to the libido in men and causes an increase of its activity. . . . When erotogenic susceptibility to stimulation has been successfully transferred by a woman from the clitoris to the vaginal orifice, it implies that she has adopted a new leading zone for the purposes of her later sexual activity. A man, on the other hand, retains his leading zone unchanged from childhood.'[2]

In one of his Two Encyclopaedia Articles (1923), Freud states: 'In the subsequent period of *puberty*, the Oedipus complex is revivified in the unconscious and embarks upon further modifications. It is only at puberty that the sexual instincts develop to their full intensity; but the direction of that development, as well as all the predispositions for it, have already been determined by the early efflorescence of sexuality during childhood which preceded it. This diphasic development of the sexual function—in two stages, interrupted by the latency period—appears to be a biological peculiarity of the human species and to contain the determining factor for the origin of neuroses.'[3]

¹ (1923e) 'The Infantile Genital Organization of the Libido', S.E., Vol. 19, p. 142.
² (1905d) *Three Essays on the Theory of Sexuality*, S.E., Vol. 7, p. 220 f.
³ (1923a) 'Two Encyclopaedia Articles', S.E., Vol. 18, p. 246, cf. also (1926f) 'Psycho-Analysis: Freudian School', S.E., Vol. 20, p. 267.

The link between early sexual development, the manner in which the oedipal conflict was resolved, and the choice of an object after puberty was examined closely by Freud in some of his writings, starting mainly with his paper 'On Narcissism' (1914) In a footnote, dated 1920, in the *Three Essays,* Freud states: 'The phantasies of the pubertal period have as their starting-point the infantile sexual researches that were abandoned in childhood. No doubt, too, they are also present before the end of the latency period. They may persist wholly, or to a great extent, unconsciously and for that reason it is often impossible to date them accurately.'[1]

In an earlier edition, in the same paper, Freud had stated: 'At the same time as these plainly incestuous fantasies are overcome and repudiated, one of the most significant, but also one of the most painful, physical achievements of the pubertal period is completed: detachment from parental authority, a process that alone makes possible the opposition, which is so important for the progress of civilization, between the new generation and the old.'[2]

Freud referred to characteristic differences in the type of object-choice between men and women as follows:

'A comparison of the male and female sexes then shows that there are fundamental differences between them in respect of their type of object-choice, although these differences are of course not universal. Complete object-love of the attachment type is, properly speaking, characteristic of the male. It displays the marked sexual overvaluation which is doubtless derived from the child's original narcissism and thus corresponds to a transference of that narcissism to the sexual object. . . . A different course is followed in the type of female most frequently met with, which is probably the pures and truest one. With the onset of puberty the maturing of the female sexual organs, which up till then have been in a condition of latency, seems to bring about an intensification of the original narcissism, and this is unfavourable to the development of a true object-choice with its accompanying sexual overvaluation.'[3]

In his paper on 'Female Sexuality' (1931), Freud again takes up the question of the finding of an object. Although his remarks are now mainly related to the child, they are relevant for the understanding of the choice, after puberty, of an object.

---

[1] [1920] (1905d) *Three Essays on the Theory of Sexuality,* S.E., Vol. 7, p. 226n.
[2] ibid., p. 227.
[3] (1914c) 'On Narcissism: an Introduction', S.E., Vol. 14, p. 88.

THE LIBIDO THEORY

'In the case of a male, his mother becomes his first love-object as a
result of her feeding him and looking after him, and she remains
so until she is replaced by someone who resembles her or is derived
from her. A female's first object, too, must be her mother: the
primary conditions for a choice of object are, of course, the same
for all children. But at the end of her development, her father—
a man—should have become her new love-object. In other words,
to the change in her own sex there must correspond a change in
the sex of her object. The new problems that now require investi-
gating are in what way this change takes place, how radically or how
incompletely it is carried out, and what the different possibilities
are which present themselves in the course of this development.'[1]

[1] (1931b) 'Female Sexuality', S.E., Vol. 21, p. 228.

AUTOEROTISM

SEE CONCEPTS: *Erotogenic Zones, Narcissism*

Autoerotism is the term used by Freud to describe a phase in libidinal development. Autoerotic is a term used to describe a specific type of sexual activity and gratification. The specific type of sexual gratification during this phase of autoerotism is autoerotic. It must be noted that autoerotic forms of gratification will continue beyond the libidinal phase of autoerotism into that of narcissism (primary) where they are still the specific form of sexual gratification. Furthermore, they are to be found sometimes side by side with the sexual gratification that characterizes the more advanced libidinal phase of object love.

Autoerotic activities are observable during early sexual development in all erotogenic zones, the major ones being mouth, anus and genitalia.

Freud's first mention of the term appears in a letter to Fliess dated December 9, 1899, where he says:

'The lowest of the sexual strata is autoerotism, which renounces any psycho-sexual aim and seeks only local gratification. This is superseded by allo-erotic (homo- and hetero-) but undoubtedly survives as an independent tendency'.[1]

Though Freud borrowed the term from Havelock Ellis who introduced it in 1898, he used it in a different sense from that of H. Ellis:

'Havelock Ellis, it is true, uses the word autoerotic in a somewhat different sense, to describe an excitation which is not provoked from outside [whether directly or indirectly] but arises internally. What psychoanalysis regards as the essential point is not the genesis of the excitation but the question of its relation to an object.'[2]

It can be said of an autoerotic activity that it is an object-less instinctual activity which consists of seeking for a particular kind of

---

[1] (1950a [1887–1902]) *The Origins of Psycho-Analysis*, Letters to Wilhelm Fliess, London, Imago, p. 303 f.
[2] [1920] (1905d) *Three Essays on the Theory of Sexuality*, S.E., Vol. 7, p. 181, n. 2.

pleasure or gratification, brought about by a special manipulation necessary to produce the gratification, calming the excitation in the corresponding erotogenic zone or of the particular component instinct which expresses itself through the appropriate erotogenic zone.

Freud was very consistent in insisting that autoerotism and autoerotic activities are 'object-less conditions'. 'In childhood, therefore, the sexual instinct is not unified and is at first without an object, that is autoerotic.'[1]

It is not always easy to determine how far this 'objectlessness' which is the main characteristic of autoerotic activities is maintained in Freud's formulation. It seems that neither the cases in which there is a physical biological dependence of a component instinct on an object in the external world, nor the cases in which there is an object choice through the agency of the ego—though mainly operative in fantasy—are truly autoerotic manifestations. That seems to be the reason for statements like the following:

'At a time at which the first beginnings of sexual satisfaction are still linked with the taking of nourishment, the sexual instinct has a sexual object outside the infant's own body in the shape of his mother's breast. It is only later that the instinct loses that object . . . As a rule the sexual instinct then becomes auto-erotic . . .'[2]

It is clear in this quotation that the object referred to is the biological object of the oral component instinct and it must be noted that Freud is quite specific: 'The sexual instinct has a sexual object outside the infant's own body.' Clearly he says that it is only later *when the instinct loses that object* that the sexual instinct becomes autoerotic.

Similarly masturbation which is accompanied by fantasies in the ego in relation to an object cannot be considered pure autoerotic activity but a highly complex composite. Freud says: 'Originally the action was a purely autoerotic procedure for the purpose of obtaining pleasure from some particularly part of the body, which could be described as erotogenic. Later, this action became merged with a wishful idea from the sphere of object-love and served as a partial realization of the situation in which the fantasy culminated.'[3] Though the physical presence of the object

[1] ibid., p. 182.   [2] ibid., p. 222.
[3] (1908a) 'Hysterical Fantasies and their Relation to Bisexuality', S.E., Vol. 9, p. 161.

is not required for the discharge, and in this sense the activity is autoerotic—since there is an object in fantasy—it becomes as Freud mentions a highly complex composite very different from the more primitive manifestations of autoerotism. This stage seems to us to be an intermediary stage in which the physical presence and body of the sexual partner is not yet necessary to achieve the necessary discharge but fantasies of the object do play an important role and are merged with the purely autoerotic activity.

Freud introduced somewhere around 1909 an intermediary stage on the way from autoerotism to object love: 'Recent investigations have directed our attention to a stage in the development of the libido, which is passed through on the way from autoerotism to object love. This stage has been given the name of narcissism. What happens is this. There comes a time in the development of the individual at which he unifies his sexual instincts (which have hitherto been engaged in autoerotic activities) in order to obtain a love-object; and he begins by taking himself, his own body, as his love object, and only subsequently proceeds from this to the choice of some person other than himself as an object'.[1]

During the phase of autoerotism each component instinct or erotogenic zone that is aroused presses for gratification quite independently of the others. According to Freud in the next stage in libidinal development (narcissism) the different component instincts get somehow unified and take the self as a love object. Consequently the type of sexual gratification during the phase of primary narcissism is autoerotic as well, the object being one's own body and not an external one as in the following phase of object love. The difference between the autoerotic activities of the phase of primary narcissism and those of autoerotism appears to be that those corresponding to primary narcissism are less close to the biological realm of phenomena than those belonging to the phase of autoerotism in which there is no awareness of the self as in primary narcissism. As Freud said 'the ego cannot exist in the individual from the start; the ego has to be developed. The auto-erotic instincts, however, are there from the very first; so there

[1] (1911c) 'Psycho-Analytic Notes on an Autobiographical Account of a Case of Paranoia (Dementia Paranoides)', S.E., Vol. 12, p. 60 f.; cf. also [1909(1905d)] *Three Essays on the Theory of Sexuality*, S.E., Vol. 7, p. 145; and (1910c) *Leonardo da Vinci and a Memory of his Childhood*, S.E., Vol. 11, p. 100.

105

must be something added to auto-erotism—a new psychical action—in order to bring about narcissism'.[1]

Finally Freud considered it important clinically that the regression in dementia praecox extends not merely to narcissism (like in paranoia) but to a complete abandonment of object love and a return to infantile autoerotism. The dispositional fixation point must therefore be situated further back than in paranoia, and must lie somewhere at the beginning of the course of development from autoerotism to object-love.[2]

[1] (1914c) 'On Narcissism: an Introduction', S.E., Vol. 14, p. 77.
[2] (1911c) 'Psycho-Analytic Notes on an Autobiographical Account of a Case of Paranoia (Dementia Paranoides)', S.E., Vol. 12, p. 77.

NARCISSISM

SEE CONCEPT: *Autoerotism*

Narcissism is the term used to describe a libidinal position inter-mediate between autoerotism and alloerotism.

The term is derived from clinical description and as Freud pointed out, was introduced by Havelock Ellis in 1898 as a description of a psychological attitude (narcissus-like) and by Paul Näcke in 1899 who used the word 'Narcismus' to describe a sexual perversion.[1]

It was on November 10, 1909, that Freud told the Vienna Society that 'narcissism was a necessary intermediate stage in the passage from autoerotism to alloerotism'.[2]

The first written accounts on narcissism appeared in a footnote, added to the second edition of the *Three Essays* dated December 1909,[3] and in Freud's book on *Leonardo* (1910).[4] Both instances refer to the finding of a love object along the path of narcissism.

The fullest description among these early accounts of the theory of narcissism appeared in the Schreber Case where Freud says: 'Recent investigations [Sadger, I. (1910) "Jb. psychoan. psychopath. Forsch.", 2, 59 and Freud's *Leonardo* (1910)] have directed our attention to a stage in the development of libido which it passes through on the way from autoerotism to object love. This stage has been given the name of narcissism. What happens is this. There comes a time in the development of the individual at which he unifies his sexual instincts (which have hitherto been engaged in autoerotic activities) in order to obtain a love-object; and he begins by taking himself, . . . as a love-object. . . . This half-way phase between autoerotism and object love may perhaps be in-dispensable normally; but it appears that many people linger un-

[1] [1915, 1920] (1905d) *Three Essays on the Theory of Sexuality*, S.E., Vol. 7, p. 218 n.3, cf. also (1914c) 'On Narcissism: an Introduction', S.E., Vol. 14, p. 73.
[2] Jones, E., *Sigmund Freud, Life and Works*, London, 1955, Vol. 2, p. 304.
[3] (1905d) *Three Essays on the Theory of Sexuality*, S.E., Vol. 7, p. 144 f., n.
[4] (1910c) *Leonardo da Vinci and a Memory of his Childhood*, S.E., Vol. 11, p. 100.

usually long in this condition, and that many of its features are carried over by them into later stages of their development. What is of chief importance in the subject's self thus chosen as a love-object may already be the genitals. The line of development then leads on to the choice of an external object with similar genitals—that is, to homosexual object choice—and thence to heterosexuality.'[1]

Later, in *Totem and Taboo* (1913) Freud stated: 'Manifestations of the sexual instincts can be observed from the very first, but to begin with they are not yet directed towards any external object. The separate instinctual components of sexuality work independently of one another to obtain pleasure and find satisfaction in the subject's own body. This stage is known as that of auto-erotism and it is succeeded by one in which an object is chosen.

'Further study has shown that it is expedient and indeed indispensable to insert a third stage between these two, [he refers here to autoerotism and alloerotism] or, putting it in another way, to divide the first stage, that of autoerotism, into two.' He goes on: 'At this intermediate stage, the importance of which is being made more and more evident by research, the hitherto isolated sexual instincts have already come together into a single whole and have also found an object. But this object is not an external one, extraneous to the subject, but it is his own ego, which has been constituted at about the same time.' A few lines later he describes the narcissistic stage as one 'at which the hitherto dissociated sexual instincts come together into a single unit and cathect the ego as an object', and on account of this 'we suspect already that this narcissistic organization is never wholly abandoned. A human being remains to some extent narcissistic even after he has found external objects for his libido'.[2]

In 'The Disposition to Obsessional Neurosis' (1913) Freud refers to the subject in very much the same terms as above and explains again how in the transition from autoerotism to narcissism the choice of an object has been made which 'coincides with the subject's own ego'.[3]

Though references to the subject of narcissism are to be found everywhere in Freud's work after the first introduction of the

---

[1] (1911c) 'Psycho-Analytic Notes on an Autobiographical Account of a Case of Paranoia (Dementia Paranoides)', S.E., Vol. 12, p. 60 f.

[2] (1912–13) *Totem and Taboo*, S.E., Vol. 13, p. 88 f.

[3] (1913i) 'The Predisposition to Obsessional Neurosis', S.E., Vol. 12, p. 321.

subject, the next really important exposition came in his paper 'On Narcissism' (1914). Here Freud again insisted on the universality of narcissism as a libidinal position: '. . . it might claim a place in the regular course of human sexual development'. (Freud here referred to a paper by Otto Rank written in 1911.)[1]

He further explained that narcissism in the sense of a libidinal position 'would not be a perversion, but the libidinal complement to the egoism of the instinct of self-preservation, a measure of which may be justifiably attributed to every living creature'.[2] On the other hand it can develop to a degree where it acquires the significance of a perversion, absorbing the whole of the subject's sexual life.[3]

In this paper Freud referred for the first time to primary and secondary narcissism. He did so in trying to describe what happens to the libido which is withdrawn from objects in processes like schizophrenia. The megalomania observable was attributed to the libido that had been withdrawn from the objects. He considered it to be no new creation but a manifestation of a condition that existed previously: 'This leads us to look upon the narcissism which arises through the drawing in of object-cathexis as a secondary one, superimposed upon a primary narcissism that is obscured by a number of different influences.'[4]

In view of all that has preceded, the following line of developmental progression and possible regression (in some cases under normal conditions such as sleep, etc., and in others under abnormal ones) can be drawn.

Autoerotism—Primary Narcissism—Object Love (homosexual and heterosexual). Withdrawal of cathexes from the objects giving place to Secondary Narcissism.

A point frequently overlooked in the literature on narcissism is Freud's attempt to make clear the differences between narcissism and the previous stage of libidinal organization: '. . . what is the relation of the narcissism of which we are now speaking to autoerotism, which we have described as an early state of the libido ?'[5] He answers that question by saying: 'I may point out that we are bound to suppose that a unity comparable to the ego cannot exist in the individual from the start; the ego has to be developed. The

[1] (1914c) 'On Narcissism: an Introduction', S.E., Vol. 14, p. 73.
[2] ibid., p. 73 f. [3] ibid., p. 73.
[4] ibid., p. 75. [5] ibid., p. 76.

autoerotic instincts, however, are there from the very first; so there must be something added to autoerotism—a new psychical action—in order to bring about narcissism.'[1]

The clinical value of the distinction made between the stage of autoerotism and that of narcissism can be summarized in the following way.

Freud attributed the dispositional fixation point of paranoia to the stage of primary narcissism and that of schizophrenia even earlier, that is, to the stage of autoerotism.[2] In Schreber's Case he clearly states (referring to schizophrenia): 'The regression extends not merely to narcissism (manifesting itself in the shape of megalomania) but to a complete abandonment of object love and a return to infantile autoerotism. The dispositional fixation must therefore be situated further back than in paranoia, and must lie somewhere at the beginning of the course of development from autoerotism to object love.'[3] In the same paper a few pages earlier he had said: '. . . it may be concluded that in paranoia the liberated libido becomes attached to the ego, and is used for the aggrandize-ment of the ego. A return is thus made to the stage of narcissism (known to us from the development of the libido), in which a person's only sexual object is his own ego.'[4]

In the *Introductory Lectures* Freud refers to the way in which the theory of narcissism made it possible to extend psychoanalytic conceptions to these other groups of diseases (i.e., dementia praecox, megalomania). He gave Abraham credit for having expressed already in 1908 (i.e. before Freud's communication to the Vienna Society) that in dementia praecox 'the libidinal cathexis of objects was lacking'. Freud continues: 'Abraham did not hesitate to give the answer: it [the libido] is turned back on to the ego and *this reflexive turning back is the source of the megalomania* in dementia praecox.'[5]

It ought to be noted that when the theory of narcissism was introduced an important modification of the theory of instincts had to take place. The duality 'ego-instincts (self-preservative)' and 'sexual instincts' had to be given up since the self-preservative

---

[1] ibid., p. 76 f. n.
[2] (1913i) 'The Predisposition to Obsessional Neurosis', S.E., Vol. 12, p. 318.
[3] (1911c) 'Psycho-Analytic Notes on an Autobiographical Account of a Case of Paranoia (Dementia Paranoides)', S.E., Vol. 12, p. 77.
[4] ibid., p. 72.
[5] (1916–17) *Introductory Lectures on Psycho-Analysis*, S.E., Vol. 16, p. 415.

instincts were identified with the sexual ones. Freud then postulated other ego instincts which he referred to as 'ego-interest' or 'interest'.

Similarly, the conflict that was until then described as being between the 'sexual' and the 'ego instincts' became now one between 'ego libido' and 'object libido': 'The opposition between the ego instincts and the sexual instincts was transformed into one between the ego instincts and the object instincts, both of a libidinal nature.'[1]

The theory of narcissism further helped to clarify other types of processes and phenomena like hypochondria, the distribution of libido in organic diseases, sleep, in conditions of intense love, as well as throwing light on the questions of object choice (anaclitic and narcissistic) and certain types of homosexuality, etc.

In view of the complexity of the subject of narcissism, a schematic chart has been attached which aims at clarifying the connections between entities such as autoerotism, primary and secondary narcissism, object libido, etc. (See next page).

[1] (1920g) *Beyond the Pleasure Principle*, S.E., Vol. 18, p. 61, n.1.

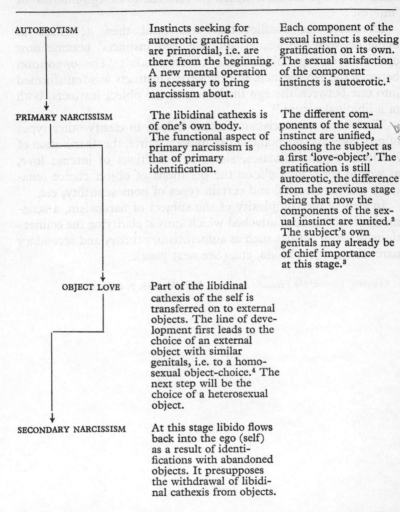

LIBIDINAL STAGES	INSTINCTUAL QUALITIES	VICISSITUDES OF COMPONENT INSTINCTS
AUTOEROTISM	Instincts seeking for autoerotic gratification are primordial, i.e. are there from the beginning. A new mental operation is necessary to bring narcissism about.	Each component of the sexual instinct is seeking gratification on its own. The sexual satisfaction of the component instincts is autoerotic.[1]
PRIMARY NARCISSISM	The libidinal cathexis is of one's own body. The functional aspect of primary narcissism is that of primary identification.	The different components of the sexual instinct are unified, choosing the subject as a first 'love-object'. The gratification is still autoerotic, the difference from the previous stage being that now the components of the sexual instinct are united.[2] The subject's own genitals may already be of chief importance at this stage.[3]
OBJECT LOVE	Part of the libidinal cathexis of the self is transferred on to external objects. The line of development first leads to the choice of an external object with similar genitals, i.e. to a homosexual object-choice.[4] The next step will be the choice of a heterosexual object.	
SECONDARY NARCISSISM	At this stage libido flows back into the ego (self) as a result of identifications with abandoned objects. It presupposes the withdrawal of libidinal cathexis from objects.	

[1] (1912–13) *Totem and Taboo*, S.E., Vol. 13, p. 88, cf. also (1911c) 'Psycho-Analytic Notes on an Autobiographical Account of a Case of Paranoia (Dementia Paranoides)', S.E., Vol. 12, p. 60 f.

[2] Ibid., Vol. 12, p. 60 f. and Vol. 13, p. 88.

[3] (1916–17) *Introductory Lectures on Psycho-Analysis*, S.E., Vol. 16, p. 314.

[4] (1911c) 'Psycho-analytic Notes on an Autobiographical Account of a Case of Paranoia (Dementia Paranoides)', S.E., Vol. 12, p. 60 f.

MASOCHISM

Masochism is the term to describe the fusion between destructiveness directed inwards and sexuality,[1] a certain amount of which is always present in normal sexual relations, though in extreme cases of perversion it causes the subject to suffer pain, ill-treatment and humiliation as the main or even sole sexual aim.[2] Freud discussed it for the first time in his *Three Essays on the Theory of Sexuality* (1905d) but his final formulations only appeared twenty years later in 'The Economic Problem of Masochism' (1924c). Three main phases can be distinguished in the development of Freud's conceptualization of masochism:

(*a*) 1905–19, when he discussed masochism almost exclusively as a perversion, as a transformation of sadism, and had serious doubts as to the existence of primary masochism.

(*b*) 1919–24, when masochism was not only seen in the light of a perversion, but as a regressive phenomenon due to an unconscious need for punishment. In 1920 the existence of primary masochism was first mentioned as a possibility.

(*c*) 1924–37, when—in connection with the theory of the death instinct—Freud postulated a primary as well as a secondary masochism and further distinguished the three forms of erotogenic, feminine, and moral masochism.

(a) *1905–19:* From the earliest formulations onwards Freud recognized the close link between masochistic tendencies and the sexual instincts, speaking of the 'masochistic components of the sexual instinct'.[3] He considered the erotogenic effects of painful feelings as one of the main roots of the masochistic-sadistic instinct.[4] He went so far as to define masochism as comprising 'any passive attitude towards sexual life and the sexual object, the extreme instance of which appears to be that in which satisfaction is conditional upon suffering physical or mental pain at the hands

---

[1] (1930a) *Civilization and its Discontents*, S.E., Vol. 21, p. 119 f.
[2] (1933a) *New Introductory Lectures on Psycho-Analysis*, S.E., Vol. 22, p. 135 f.
[3] (1900a) *The Interpretation of Dreams*, S.E., Vol. 4–5, p. 159; cf. also (1905d) *Three Essays on the Theory of Sexuality*, S.E., Vol. 7, p. 150 n.
[4] (1905d) *Three Essays on the Theory of Sexuality*, S.E., Vol. 7, p. 204.

H

of the sexual object'.[1] These extreme cases are to be considered as perversions which are the result of the exaggeration and fixation of the original passive sexual aim.[2]

But even as perversions both sadism and masochism occupy a special position 'since the contrast between activity and passivity which lies behind them is among the universal characteristics of sexual life'.[3] Both the active and the passive forms of this perversion are habitually found in the same individual. Hence a sadist is always at the same time a masochist.[4] This is not only due to the element of aggressiveness but also to bisexuality.[5] The realization that there are sadistic and masochistic perverts who are capable of substituting a phantasy for real sexual satisfaction[6] marked an important step forward towards Freud's later formulations.

During this period Freud expressed his serious doubts as to whether masochism could be a primary phenomenon.[7] He rather thought that masochism always came into existence as a reversal of an aggressive, sadistic component into its opposite.[8] In 1905 he defined masochism as the 'passive instinct of cruelty,[9] and in 1915 we find the formulation that 'masochism is actually sadism turned round upon the subject's own ego', the essence of the process being the change of the object.[10] It is important to note that at this time Freud did not include self-torture and self-punishment under masochism,[11] whereas later they were considered as among the main characteristics of moral masochism. He further maintained that the reversal from activity to passivity and the turning round upon the subject involved in the transformation of sadism into masochism never 'involves the whole quota of the instinctual impulse'[12] and that the transformation 'implies a return to the

[1] ibid., p. 158.
[2] ibid., p. 158 f.
[3] ibid., p. 159.
[4] ibd., pp. 159, 167.
[5] ibid., p. 160.
[6] (1916–17) *Introductory Lectures on Psycho-Analysis*, S.E., Vol. 15–16, p. 257 f.
[7] (1905d) *Three Essays on the Theory of Sexuality*, S.E., Vol. 7, p. 158; cf. also (1915c) 'Instincts and their Vicissitudes', S.E., Vol. 14, p. 128.
[8] (1900a) *The Interpretation of Dreams*, S.E., Vol. 4–5, p. 159; cf. also (1905d) *Three Essays on the Theory of Sexuality*, S.E., Vol. 7, p. 158.
[9] (1905d) *Three Essays on the Theory of Sexuality*, S.E., Vol. 7, p. 193.
[10] (1915c) 'Instincts and their Vicissitudes', S.E. Vol. 14, p. 127.
[11] ibid., p. 128.
[12] ibid., p. 130.

narcissistic object'.[1] The enjoyment of pain is an aim 'which was originally masochistic, but which can only become an instinctual aim in someone who was originally sadistic'. This is probably due to the fact that the causing of pain is enjoyed masochistically by the subject through identification with the suffering object.[2]

(b) *1919–24:* The paper 'A Child is Being Beaten' (1919e)—a study of beating-fantasies among boys and girls—contains many new insights into the problem of masochism. Freud himself referred to it as a paper on masochism.[3] In it he postulated that a sense of guilt is invariably the factor that transforms sadism into masochism, and that sexual love contributes an important share to its content.[4] It is this sense of guilt which, in certain patients, finds its satisfaction in the illness, and refuses to give up the punishment of suffering.[5] He characterized one form of masochism in the following way: '*It is not only the punishment for the forbidden genital relation, but also the regressive substitute for that relation,* and from this latter source it derives the libidinal excitation which is from this time forward attached to it.'[6] Although the form of such a beating-fantasy is sadistic, the satisfaction derived from it is masochistic because the libidinal cathexis of the repressed portion of the fantasy and the sense of guilt attached to that portion have been taken over.[7] In both sexes the masochistic fantasy of being beaten by the father lives on in the unconscious after repression.[8]

In 1919 Freud still held fast to the view that 'masochism is not the manifestation of a primary instinct, but originates from sadism which has been turned round upon the self—that is to say, by means of regression from an object to the ego'.[9] There is, however, already an allusion to what was later distinguished as 'feminine masochism' when Freud postulated the existence—especially among women—of instincts with a passive aim.[10]

In *Beyond the Pleasure Principle* (1920g) we find the first mention of two ideas which were fully developed in the paper on masochism four years later, namely that there are masochistic

---

[1] ibid., p. 132.   [2] ibid., p. 129.
[3] (1919e) 'A Child is Being Beaten', S.E., Vol. 17, p. 177.
[4] ibid., p. 189.
[5] (1923b) *The Ego and the Id*, S.E., Vol. 19, p. 49 f.
[6] (1919e) 'A Child is Being Beaten', S.E., Vol. 17, p. 189.
[7] ibid., p. 190 f.   [8] ibid., p. 198 f.
[9] ibid., p. 193 f.   [10] ibid., p. 193 f.

trends of the ego[1] and that there might be such a thing as primary masochism.[2]

(c) *1924–37.* The paper on 'The Economic Problem of Masochism' (1924c) contains Freud's final formulations as regards this concept. He now differentiated two types: primary and secondary masochism; and three forms: an erotogenic masochism, out of which two later forms, feminine and moral masochism, develop.[3]

Erotogenic masochism. This is the primary masochism[4] which has a biological and constitutional basis[5] and is defined as pleasure in pain.[6] For all practical purposes it is identical with the death instinct (primal sadism) and is that portion of this instinct which has not been transposed outwards onto objects but has remained inside fused with the libido, with the self as its object. Erotogenic or primary masochism is evidence of the coalescence and fusion between the death instinct and Eros.[7] It 'accompanies the libido through all its developmental phases and derives from them its changing psychical coatings'.[8]

Feminine masochism. This is the least problematical form and the one most accessible to observation.[9] It is called feminine because the fantasies associated with it place the subject in a characteristically female situation of being castrated, copulated with, or giving birth to a baby. Many of its features also point to infantile life in that the masochist wants to be treated like a small, helpless, naughty child.[10] The condition that the suffering has to emanate from a loved person is essential.[11]

Moral Masochism. This is the most important form which is determined by a mostly unconscious sense of guilt or need for punishment.[12] It has loosened its connection with sexuality in that the suffering in itself is what matters, with the object being irrelevant.[13] Moral masochism has to be clearly distinguished from an

[1] (1920g) *Beyond the Pleasure Principle,* S.E., Vol. 18, p. 13 f.
[2] ibid., p. 54 f.
[3] (1905d) *Three Essays on the Theory of Sexuality,* S.E., Vol. 7; cf. also (1924c) 'The Economic Problem of Masochism', S.E., Vol. 19, p. 161.
[4] (1905d) *Three Essays on the Theory of Sexuality,* S.E., Vol. 7, p. 158.
[5] (1924c) 'The Economic Problem of Masochism', S.E., Vol. 19, p. 161.
[6] ibid., p. 162.   [7] ibid., pp. 164, 170.
[8] ibid., p. 164 f.   [9] ibid., p. 161.
[10] ibid., p. 162.   [11] ibid., p. 164.
[12] ibid., pp. 161, 166, 169; cf. (1937c) 'Analysis Terminable and Interminable, S.E., Vol. 23, p. 242 f.
[13] (1924c) 'The Economic Problem of Masochism', S.E., Vol. 19, p. 165.

unconscious extension of morality, which is characterized by the ego's submission to the heightened sadism of the superego, while in moral masochism it is the ego's own, largely unconscious masochism, which seeks punishment from the superego or authoritative external powers. In moral masochism the sadism of the superego and the masochism of the ego supplement each other and produce the same effect. Beating-fantasies are a regressive distortion of the wish to have passive, feminine sexual relations with the father, and constitute the hidden meaning of moral masochism, which at the same time leads to a resexualization of morality and to a revival of the Oedipus complex.[1]

Secondary masochism. This is produced by the instinct of destruction which cannot find employment as sadism in actual life, retreats and is turned round upon the subject's own self, where part of it is superadded to the primary masochism, whereas another part is taken up by the superego, thus increasing its sadism.[2] This turning back of sadism against the self occurs particularly where cultural suppression of the instincts holds back a large part of the subject's destructive instinctual components from being exercised in life.[3]

Feminine and moral masochism are not to be considered as primary masochism, although Freud is not explicit about this. It is also implicit in his formulations that both can be increased by secondary masochism.

In his later works Freud clarified some further aspects in regard to masochism. He stated that masochistic impulses get reinforced by regression and can be the cause for new symptoms in obsessional neuroses.[4] Exaggerated anxiety-reactions in the face of real danger situations can be understood as a summation of realistic anxiety and anxiety caused by the instinct of destruction directed against the subject himself.[5] Freud also maintained that complete masochists need not necessarily be neurotic.[6] He further clarified the point that masochism is only to be called a perversion when it thrusts the other sexual aims into the background and

[1] ibid., p. 169.
[2] (1905d) *Three Essays on the Theory of Sexuality*, S.E., Vol. 7, p. 158; cf. also (1924c) 'The Economic Problem of Masochism', S.E., Vol. 19, pp. 164, 170.
[3] (1924c) 'The Economic Problem of Masochism', S.E., Vol. 19, p. 170.
[4] (1926d) *Inhibitions, Symptoms and Anxiety*, S.E., Vol. 20, p. 117.
[5] ibid., p. 168 n.
[6] (1928b) 'Dostoevsky and Parricide', S.E., Vol. 21, p. 179.

substitutes its own aims for it. Sadism and masochism are corner-stones for the theory of aggression and destructiveness, and Freud argues that masochism is older than sadism, as the latter only comes into existence when the greater portion of the instinct of self-destruction (equated with masochism without its erotic components) is turned outwards. The destructive instinct is only observable when it is bound up with erotic instincts to form masochism or when it is turned outwards as aggressiveness.[1]

[1] (1933a) *New Introductory Lectures on Psycho-Analysis*, S.E., Vol. 22, p. 135 f.

SADISM

SEE CONCEPT: *Masochism*

Sadism was the term used to describe a desire to humiliate, subjugate and/or to inflict pain, etc., upon the sexual object, which reaches its height in the classic perversion but an element of which is present in normal sexuality.

Initially, Freud viewed sadism as one of the component instincts of the sexual instinct. He kept to this view until the formulation of a death instinct, when he considered sadism in relation to the aggressive instinct. But it is to be remarked that even there, and in Freud's later writings (for instance, in Chapter IV of *The Ego and the Id*), the aggressive instinct was still something secondary, derived from the primary self-destructive death instinct.[1]

Freud's first detailed discussion of sadism is in the *Three Essays on the Theory of Sexuality*. 'As regards algolagnia, sadism, the roots are easy to detect in the normal. The sexuality of most male human beings contains an element of aggressiveness—a desire to subjugate; the biological significance of it seems to lie in the need for overcoming the resistance of the sexual object by means other than the process of wooing. Thus sadism would correspond to an aggressive component of the sexual instinct which has become independent and exaggerated and, by displacement, has usurped the leading position.'[2]

Sadism was originally thought to be the active part in the pair of component instincts sadism-masochism. It must be noted that though sadism was considered as a component of the sexual instinct, masochism was on the other hand, to start with, described by Freud not as a primary phenomenon but the result of the turning against the self of sadism. 'Sadism and masochism occupy a special position among the perversions, since the contrast between activity and passivity which lies behind them is among the universal characteristics of sexual life.'[3]

[1] [Editor's Introduction] (1923b) *The Ego and the Id*, S.E., Vol. 19, p. 3 f.
[2] (1905d) *Three Essays on the Theory of Sexuality*, S.E., Vol. 7, p. 157 f.
[3] [1915] (1905d) ibid., p. 159.

'It is, moreover, a suggestive fact that the existence of the pair of opposites formed by sadism and masochism cannot be attributed merely to the element of aggressiveness. We should rather be inclined to connect the simultaneous presence of these opposites with the opposing masculinity and femininity which are combined in bisexuality—a contrast which often has to be replaced in psychoanalysis by that between activity and passivity.'[1] (The editor's footnote points out that the last clause is the 1924 version of Freud's. It is important to note this because by this time Freud had postulated the life and death instincts, and it was the time just after the structural theory was put forward in *The Ego and the Id*.)

In the analysis of melancholia, Freud shows how it is possible for one to treat oneself as an object, and in this sense turn the sadism against one's own ego, even to the point of killing oneself. 'The analysis of melancholia now shows that the ego can kill itself only if, owing to the return of the object-cathexis, it can treat itself as an object—if it is able to direct against itself the hostility which relates to an object and which represents the ego's original reaction to objects in the external world.'[2]

It was in *Beyond the Pleasure Principle* (1920g), with the formulation of life and death instincts, that Freud queried his earlier assumptions in relation to sadism and masochism, and as a component instinct of the sexual instinct. He now re-examined the question of sadism in relation to the death instinct, accepting primary masochism as a possibility. When this primary masochism is turned outside it becomes sadism. (See 'Masochism' for full description.)

Freud pointed out that in sadism—as a perversion—both its active (sadism) and its passive form (masochism) always occur together, though the one or the other element of the pair may predominate. In a footnote added in 1924 to the *Three Essays*, Freud refers to his having been 'led to assign a peculiar position, based upon the origin of the instincts, to the pair of opposites constituted by sadism and masochism, and to place them outside the class of the remaining perversions'.[3]

'From the very first we recognized the presence of a sadistic

[1] [1924] (1905d) ibid., p. 160.
[2] (1917e [1915]) 'Mourning and Melancholia', S.E., Vol. 14, p. 252.
[3] [1924] (1905d) *Three Essays on the Theory of Sexuality*, S.E., Vol. 7, p. 159, n. 2.

component in the sexual instinct. As we know, it can make itself independent and can, in the form of a perversion, dominate an individual's entire sexual activity. It also emerges as a predominant component instinct in one of the "pregenital organizations", as I have named them. But how can the sadistic instinct, whose aim it is to injure the object, be derived from Eros, the preserver of life? Is it not plausible to suppose that this sadism is in fact a death instinct which, under the influence of the narcissistic libido, has been forced away from the ego and has consequently only emerged in relation to the object? It now enters the service of the sexual function. During the oral stage of organization of the libido, the act of obtaining erotic mastery over an object coincides with that object's destruction; later, the sadistic instinct separates off, and finally, at the stage of genital primacy, it takes on, for the purposes of reproduction, the function of overpowering the sexual object to the extent necessary for carrying out the sexual act. It might indeed be said that the sadism which has been forced out of the ego has pointed the way for the libidinal components of the sexual instinct, and that these follow after it to the object. Wherever the original sadism has undergone no mitigation or intermixture, we find the familiar ambivalence of love and hate in erotic life.'[1]

The following most important proposition was put forward by Freud and rounds up his final views on the matter. 'It is our opinion, then, that in sadism and in masochism we have before us two excellent examples of a mixture of the two classes of instinct, of Eros and aggressiveness; and we proceed to the hypothesis that this relation is a model one—that every instinctual impulse that we can examine consists of similar fusions or alloys of the two classes of instinct.'[2]

In 'The Economic Problem of Masochism', Freud examines in detail the question of the existence of a primary masochism, but this in turn necessitates examining the question of sadism as well. 'The libido has the task of making the destroying instinct innocuous, and it fulfils the task by diverting that instinct to a great extent outwards—soon with the help of a special organic system, the muscular apparatus—towards objects in the external world. The instinct is then called the destructive instinct, the instinct for mastery, or the will to power. A portion of the instinct is placed

---

[1] (1920g) *Beyond the Pleasure Principle*, S.E., Vol. 18, p. 53 f.
[2] (1933a) *New Introductory Lectures on Psycho-Analysis*, S.E., Vol. 22, p. 104.

directly in the service of the sexual function, where it has an important part to play. This is sadism proper.'[1]

'If one is prepared to overlook a little inexactitude, it may be said that the death instinct which is operative in the organism—primal sadism—is identical with masochism.'[2]

[1] (1924c) 'The Economic Problem of Masochism', S.E., Vol. 19, p. 163.
[2] ibid., p. 164.

BISEXUALITY

1. Definition

Bisexuality is a biological concept,[1] and 'psycho-analysis has a common basis with biology, in that it presupposes an original bisexuality in human beings (as in animals). But psycho-analysis cannot elucidate the intrinsic nature of what in conventional or in biological phraseology is termed "masculine" and "feminine": it simply takes over the two concepts and makes them the foundation of its work.'[2] In psychoanalysis, bisexuality—universally to be found in the innate constitution of every human being[3]—refers to the tendency of human beings to distribute their libido 'either in a manifest or a latent fashion, over objects of both sexes'.[4]

Evidence of the universality of bisexuality can be found both on a physical and on a mental level. With regard to the former, Freud maintains that 'a certain degree of anatomical hermaphroditism occurs normally', i.e. traces are found in every individual of the apparatus of the opposite sex.[5] On a mental level, bisexuality manifests itself in a 'masculine or feminine attitude', neither of

[1] (1950a) *The Origins of Psycho-Analysis*, S.E., Vol. 1, p. 326 f. (cf. different and more accurate translation of passage in S.E., Vol. 7, p. 4); (1905d) *Three Essays on Sexuality*, Vol. 7, p. 141; (1905e) 'Fragment of an Analysis of a Case of Hysteria', S.E., Vol. 7, p. 113 f.; (1910c) *Leonardo da Vinci*, S.E., Vol. 11, p. 136; (1940a [1938]) *An Outline of Psycho-Analysis*, S.E., Vol. 23, p. 188.

[2] (1920a) 'The Psychogenesis of a Case of Female Homosexuality', S.E., Vol. 18, p. 171; (1933a) *New Introductory Lectures on Psycho-Analysis*, S.E., Vol. 22, p. 114.

[3] (1950a) *The Origins of Psycho-Analysis*, S.E., Vol. 1, p. 179; (1920a) 'The Psychogenesis of a Case of Female Homosexuality', S.E., Vol. 18, p. 156 f.; (1923b) *The Ego and the Id*, S.E., Vol. 19, p. 31; (1925d) *An Autobiographical Study*, S.E., Vol. 20, p. 36; (1925j) 'Some Psychological Consequences of the Anatomical Distinction Between the Sexes', S.E., Vol. 19, p. 258; (1928b) 'Dostoevsky and Parricide', S.E., Vol. 21, p. 183 f.; (1930a) *Civilization and its Discontents*, S.E., Vol. 21, p. 105 f.; n. 3; (1931b) 'Female Sexuality', S.E., Vol. 21, p. 227 f.

[4] (1937c) 'Analysis Terminable and Interminable', S.E., Vol. 23, p. 274.

[5] (1905d) *Three Essays on the Theory of Sexuality*, S.E., Vol. 7, p. 141; (1920a) 'The Psychogenesis of a Case of Female Homosexuality', S.E., Vol. 18, p. 170; (1933a) *New Introductory Lectures on Psycho-Analysis*, S.E., Vol. 22, p. 114.

which are found in pure form in any individual,[1] but show themselves in the reactions of human beings which are all 'made up of masculine and feminine traits',[2] and in a mixture of character-traits belonging to both sexes.[3]

2. Historical Development

Freud took over the idea of a constitutional bisexuality from Fliess in the 1890s and soon recognized the important contribution which this concept could make to the understanding of the neuroses.[4] Around the turn of the century Freud even intended to write a book on the 'Bisexuality in Man'.[5] Freud's views and formulations with regard to bisexuality remained consistent throughout his writings, with one important exception. Both Freud and Fliess originally held bisexuality 'responsible for the inclination to repression'.[6] In 1901 Freud still maintained that repression 'is only possible through reaction between two sexual impulses'[7] and that repression presupposes bisexuality[8]; furthermore, in 1905, he held the bisexual constitution responsible for the existence of the pair of opposites formed by sadism and masochism.[9] But in 1914 Freud explicitly repudiated the general validity of his and Fliess' original hypothesis: 'To insist that bisexuality is the motive force leading to repression is to take too narrow a view'. At the same time he stated clearly that in many instances it is the ego which puts the repression into operation, 'for the benefit of one of the sexual tendencies'.[10]

Although Freud considered the concept of bisexuality as one of the clinical postulates of psycho-analysis,[11] he wrote as late as 1930 that the 'theory of bisexuality is still surrounded by many ob-

---

[1] [1915] (1905d) Three Essays on the Theory of Sexuality, S.E., Vol. 7, p. 219 f. (1920a) 'The Psychogenesis of a Case of Female Homosexuality', S.E., Vol. 18, p. 170; (1925j) 'Some Psychological Consequences of the Anatomical Distinction between the Sexes', S.E., Vol. 19, p. 258.

[2] (1925j) 'Some Psychological Consequences of the Anatomical Distinction between the Sexes', S.E., Vol. 19, p. 255.

[3] [1915] (1905d) Three Essays on the Theory of Sexuality, S.E., Vol. 7, p. 219 f.

[4] (1950a) The Origins of Psycho-Analysis, S.E., Vol. 1, p. 38.

[5] ibid., p. 334 f.   [6] ibid., p. 242.

[7] ibid., p. 334 f.   [8] ibid., p. 337.

[9] (1905d) Three Essays on the Theory of Sexuality, S.E., Vol. 7, p. 160.

[10] (1918b) 'From the History of an Infantile Neurosis', S.E., Vol. 17, p. 110; (1919e) 'A Child is Being Beaten', S.E., Vol. 17, p. 200–2; (1937c) 'Analysis Terminable and Interminable', S.E., Vol. 23, p. 250 f.

[11] (1913j) 'The Claims of Psycho-Analysis to Scientific Interest', S.E., Vol. 13, p. 182.

scurities' and felt it as a particular impediment that no link with the theory of instincts had been found.[1] In his subsequent writings he threw no new light on these obscurities, nor did he establish the missing link.

3. Bisexuality and the Libido Theory

The concept of bisexuality played an important part in the development of Freud's libido theory. Already in a letter to Fliess he had written that he was accustoming himself 'to the idea of regarding every sexual act as a process in which four persons are involved'.[2] He stated that a person's sexual constitution is derived from his initial bisexuality,[3] and that normal sexual manifestations cannot be understood without taking bisexuality into account.[4] 'In all of us, throughout life, the libido normally oscillates between male and female objects.'[5] He considered bisexuality as an important aetiological precondition of neuroses whose precipitating causes he saw in external 'frustrations and internal conflicts: conflicts between the three major psychical agencies, conflicts arising within the libidinal economy in consequence of our bisexual disposition and conflicts between the erotic and the aggressive instinctual components'.[6] Bisexuality comes to the fore much more clearly in women because they have two leading sexual organs, namely the clitoris and the vagina, which divide their sexual life into two phases. The first of these has a masculine character (clitoridal sexuality, masturbation) and only the second is specifically feminine. There is nothing analogous to such a diphasic sexual development in the man as he has only one leading sexual zone.[7]

4. Bisexuality and Dreams

Freud accepts the fact that 'the tendency of dreams and of unconscious phantasies to employ sexual symbols bisexually betrays an archaic characteristic. . . . But it is possible, too, to be misled

[1] (1930a) *Civilization and Its Discontents*, S.E., Vol. 21, p. 105 f., n.3.
[2] (1950a) *The Origins of Psycho-Analysis*, S.E., Vol. 1, p. 289.
[3] (1900a) *The Interpretation of Dreams*, S.E., Vol. 4–5, p. 605 f.
[4] (1905d) *Three Essays on the Theory of Sexuality*, S.E., Vol. 7, p. 219 f.
[5] (1920a) 'The Psychogenesis of a Case of Female Homosexuality', S.E., Vol. 18, p. 158.
[6] (1931a) 'Libidinal Types', S.E., Vol. 21, p. 220.
[7] (1925j) 'Some Psychological Consequences of the Anatomical Distinction between the Sexes', S.E., Vol. 19, p. 255; (1931b) 'Female Sexuality', S.E., Vol. 21, p. 227 f.

into wrongly supposing that a sexual symbol is bisexual, if one forgets that in some dreams there is a general inversion of sex, so that what is male is represented as female and *vice versa.*'[1] In a 1911 addition to *The Interpretation of Dreams*, Freud states that 'we can assert of many dreams . . . that they are bisexual, since they unquestionably admit of an "over-interpretation" in which the dreamer's homosexual impulses are realized—impulses, that is, which are contrary to his normal sexual activities. To maintain, however, as do Stekel . . . and Adler . . . that *all* dreams are to be interpreted bisexually appears to me to be a generalization which is equally undemonstrable and unplausible and which I am not prepared to support.'[2]

5. *Bisexuality and the Oedipus Complex* (see also concept on the Oedipus Complex)

Freud put great emphasis on the importance of bisexuality with regard to the Oedipus complex. (*a*) It determines the outcome of the Oedipal situation: 'in both sexes the relative strength of the masculine and feminine sexual dispositions is what determines whether the outcome of the Oedipus situation shall be an identification with the father or with the mother. This is one of the ways in which bisexuality takes a hand in the subsequent vicissitudes of the Oedipus complex.'[3] (*b*) It is responsible for the more complete (positive and negative) Oedipus complex: 'the simple Oedipus complex is by no means its commonest form. . . . Closer study usually discloses the more complete Oedipus complex, which is twofold, positive and negative, and is due to the bisexuality originally present in children: that is to say, a boy has not merely an ambivalent attitude towards his father and an affectionate object-choice towards his mother, but at the same time he also behaves like a girl and displays an affectionate feminine attitude to his father and a corresponding jealousy and hostility towards his mother. It is this complicating element introduced by bisexuality that makes it so difficult to obtain a clear view of the facts in connection with the earliest object-choices and identifications. . . . It may even be that the ambivalence displayed in the relations to the

---

[1] [1911] [1925] (1900a) *The Interpretation of Dreams*, S.E., Vol. 4-5, p. 359.
[2] [1911] ibid., p. 396.
[3] (1923b) *The Ego and the Id*, S.E., Vol. 19, p. 33.

parents should be attributed entirely to bisexuality and that it is not . . . developed out of identification in consequence of rivalry.'[1] (c) At the dissolution of the Oedipus complex, bisexuality determines the relative strength of the identifications: 'At the dissolution of the Oedipus complex the four trends of which it consists will group themselves in such a way as to produce a father-identification and a mother-identification. . . . The relative intensity of the two identifications in any individual will reflect the preponderance in him of one or other of the two sexual dispositions.'[2]

6. Bisexuality and Neurosis

A 'strong innate bisexual disposition becomes one of the pre-conditions or reinforcements of neurosis',[3] and the strength of such a disposition is 'especially clearly visible in the analysis of psychoneurotics'.[4] The revival of repressed sexual impulses from infancy during later developmental periods may ultimately be due to our initial bisexuality, and they are 'able to furnish the motive force for the formation of psychoneurotic symptoms of every kind'.[5] Freud saw bisexuality as one of the organic bases of hysterical symptoms[6] and he postulated a 'bisexual nature of hysterical symptoms' in so far as they are the expression of both a masculine and a feminine unconscious fantasy. He did not, however, claim general validity for this formula.[7] But he emphasized the importance of realizing that a symptom may have a bisexual meaning so that it may 'persist undiminished although we have already resolved one of its sexual meanings'.[8] Jealousy, for instance, can be intensified and become neurotic if it is experienced bisexually, i.e. when a man does 'not only feel pain about the woman he loves and hatred of the man who is his rival, but also grief about the man, whom he loves unconsciously, and hatred of the woman as his rival'.[9]

[1] ibid., p. 33; (1925d) An Autobiographical Study, S.E., Vol. 20, p. 36; (1925j) 'Some Psychological Consequences of the Anatomical Distinction between the Sexes', S.E., Vol. 19, p. 249 f.
[2] (1923b) The Ego and the Id, S.E., Vol. 19, p. 34.
[3] (1928b) 'Dostoevsky and Parricide', S.E., Vol. 21, p. 184.
[4] (1908a) 'Hysterical Fantasies and their Relation to Bisexuality', S.E., Vol. 9, p. 165 f.
[5] (1900a) The Interpretation of Dreams, S.E., Vol. 5, p. 605 f.
[6] (1905e) 'Fragment of an Analysis of a Case of Hysteria', S.E., Vol. 7, p. 113 f.
[7] (1908a) 'Hysterical Fantasies and their Relation to Bisexuality', S.E., Vol. 9, p. 164–6.　[8] ibid., p. 166.
[9] (1922b) 'Some Neurotic Mechanisms in Jealousy, Paranoia and Homo sexuality', S.E., Vol. 18, p. 223.

7. *Bisexuality and Perversion*

Inversion cannot be explained as psychical hermaphroditism, i.e. it is on the whole independent of somatic hermaphroditism. However, Freud held the view that 'a bisexual disposition is somehow concerned in inversion' and affects the 'sexual instinct in the course of development'.[1] The sexual object of an invert is someone who 'combines the characters of both sexes'[2] and is thus 'a kind of reflection of the subject's own bisexual nature'.[3]

8. *Bisexuality and Conflict*

In 'Analysis Terminable and Interminable'. Freud deals with the problem why the majority of human beings cannot choose objects of either sex without interference of one trend with the other, in spite of the universality of our bisexual constitution. 'It is not clear why the rivals do not always divide up the available quota of libido between them according to their relative strength', unless one assumes an 'independently-emerging tendency to conflict' which is due to 'the intervention of an element of free aggressiveness'.[4]

[1] ibid., p. 143 f. (1925d) *An Autobiographical Study*, S.E., Vol. 20, p. 38.
[2] (1905d) *Three Essays on the Theory of Sexuality*, S.E., Vol. 7, p. 144.
[3] [1915] ibid., p. 144.
[4] (1937c) 'Analysis Terminable and Interminable', S.E., Vol. 23, p. 244.

ACTIVITY—PASSIVITY; MASCULINITY —FEMININITY

SEE CONCEPTS: *Bisexuality and Oedipus Complex*

Definition
'Activity and Passivity' and 'Masculinity and Femininity' are two aspects of psychological sexuality. Using these terms as they have been gradually developed and defined by Freud, it can be said that 'activity and passivity' is a polarity which relates to the aims of instincts, while 'masculinity and femininity' is a more complex polarity which primarily relates to the choice of the post-Oedipal sexual object and the corresponding predominance of active or passive wishes towards that object.

Freud shows that in the pre-Oedipal stages of development both boys and girls have active and passive instinctual aims, and in these stages the nature of the attachment to objects and the variations in object relationships depend more on the child's phase of development and instinctual aims than on whether the child is a boy or a girl.

Both boys and girls, therefore, have active and passive, oral, anal and phallic wishes, but during the phallic phase the sex of the child begins to play a more decisive part; the boy becomes aware that females have no penis, i.e. are 'castrated', and the girl becomes aware that her erotogenic organ, the clitoris, is inferior to and no real substitute for the penis.

In the Oedipal phase and its resolution, these anatomical facts play a significant part in differentiating the psychological development of boys from girls. The Oedipus complex offers the boy two main possibilities of satisfaction, an active wish towards the mother which would involve usurping the father's place, or a passive wish towards the father involving taking the mother's place. As the gratification of either wish invokes the threat of castration, the boy's narcissistic cathexis of his penis impels his ego to turn away from both parents and from the Oedipal complex.

The girl's development is different: in the Oedipal phase her lack of a penis induces her to repress her active phallic wishes and

I   129 to substitute the wish for a child in place of the wish for a penis; with this purpose in view, she turns away from her mother who becomes an object of jealousy, and takes instead her father as a love-object. There is not, therefore, in girls the same decisive turning away from the Oedipal complex as a whole as there is in boys.

In puberty the sexual polarity coincides with masculinity and femininity. Masculinity combines the factors of subject, activity, and possession of the penis, and the boy's development therefore continues in line with his earlier phallic development. Femininity combines the factors of object and passivity; here the girl's development is not in line with her earlier phallic development, and Freud suggests that the first phase of puberty in the girl necessitates a new measure of repression against her earlier clitoridal (phallic) sexuality in order that the vagina may become her main sexual zone and subserve the passive wish to be given a child which thus establishes her feminine sexuality.

There are numerous cases of adults, however, where there is a divergence from the normal development in respect to the sexual object and the predominant sexual aim, i.e. there is not the full masculine or feminine correspondence. To show the nature of both these factors it is necessary to differentiate between

(a) active-homosexual
(b) passive-homosexual
(c) active-heterosexual
(d) passive-heterosexual
} instinctual aim and object-choice

Historical Development

In the *Three Essays on Sexuality* (1905), Freud refers to the fact that 'certain among the impulses to perversion occur regularly as pairs of opposites; and this ... has a high theoretical significance. It is, moreover, a suggestive fact that the existence of the pair of opposites formed by sadism and masochism cannot be attributed merely to the element of aggressiveness. We should rather be inclined to connect the simultaneous presence of these opposites with the opposing masculinity and femininity which are combined in bisexuality'. A development in Freud's thinking is shown by the fact that a clause was added in the 1915 edition, saying: '—a contrast whose significance is reduced in psycho-analysis to that between activity and passivity'. In 1924, the wording of this added clause was slightly modified, not, however, its content.[1]

These changes show that Freud increasingly saw the contrast between masculinity and femininity in terms of activity versus passivity. In this sense, the psychoanalytic distinction between masculinity and femininity as a developmental process is in contrast to the layman's assessment of a difference either based on the physical sexual characteristics which are usually present and apparent at birth, or of a difference based on environmental social factors. Freud makes it quite explicit that physical sexual characteristics do not parallel mental characteristics or sexual attitudes and behaviour.[2]

Later in the same paper, Freud states that the antithesis active-passive developmentally precedes that of masculine-feminine: 'A second pre-genital phase is that of the sadistic-anal organization. Here the opposition between two currents, which runs through all sexual life, is already developed: they cannot yet, however, be described as "masculine" and "feminine" but only as "active" and "passive". The *activity* is put into operation by the instinct for mastery through the agency of the somatic musculature; the organ which, more than any other, represents the *passive* sexual aim is the erotogenic mucous membrane of the anus. Both of these currents have objects, which, however, are not identical. Alongside these, other component instincts operate in an autoerotic manner. In this phase, therefore, sexual polarity and an extraneous object are already observable. But organization and subordination to the reproductive function are still absent.'[3]

Although the case-history of Dora was also published in 1905, it was written in 1901 and already refers to the problem of bisexuality: 'Her declaration that she had been able to keep abreast with her brother up to the time of her first illness, but that after that she had fallen behind him in her studies, was in a certain sense also a "screen memory". It was as though she had been a boy up till that moment, and had then become girlish for the first time. She had in truth been a wild creature; but after the "asthma" she became quiet and well-behaved. That illness formed the boundary

---

[1](1905d) *Three Essays on the Theory of Sexuality*, S.E., Vol, 7, p. 160 and n?
[2] ibid., p. 141 f.   [3] ibid., p. 198.

between two phases of her sexual life, of which the first was masculine in character, and the second feminine.'[1]

In the *Three Essays* Freud also examines the question of sexual development and bisexuality in detail, and states that at the stage of the primacy of the genital zone, 'the new sexual aim assigns very different functions to the two sexes, [so] their sexual development now diverges greatly. That of males is the more straightforward and the more understandable, while that of females actually enters upon a kind of involution'.[2] 'As we all know, it is not until puberty that the sharp distinction is established between the masculine and feminine characters. . . . The auto-erotic activity of the erotogenic zones . . . [has been] the same in both sexes, and owing to this uniformity there is no possibility of a distinction between the two sexes such as arises after puberty. So far as the auto-erotic and masturbatory manifestations of sexuality are concerned, we might lay it down that the sexuality of little girls is of a wholly masculine character.'[3]

Freud states that the clitoris is the leading erotogenic zone of little girls at the time when their sexual development still parallels that of boys; and that later, in puberty, while there is a great accession of libido in boys, there is in girls a fresh wave of repression directed towards their clitoridal, masculine sexuality. Ideally, when the girl reaches full maturity, the last function of the clitoris should be to transmit the sexual excitation to the vagina, which should then remain the main erotogenic zone in sexual intercourse. A man, however, retains his leading erotogenic zone [the penis] unchanged from childhood, nor is there a wave of repression at puberty directed towards his masculine sexuality.[4]

Clinical material, illustrating the vicissitudes of male and female sexual development, is given in 'The Taboo of Virginity' (1918) where Freud shows that the girl's childhood 'envy for the penis' is associated with strong hostile feelings towards the more fortunate boys, and that it is only later that the wish for a penis becomes the wish for a child, and that the earlier masculine constellation may be reactivated by the first act of intercourse;[5] and in the Schreber

---

[1] (1905e[1901]) 'Fragment of an Analysis of a Case of Hysteria', S.E., Vol. 7, p. 82 n. 1.
[2] (1905d) *Three Essays on the Theory of Sexuality*, S.E., Vol. 7, p. 207.
[3] ibid., p. 219.
[4] ibid., p. 220 f.
[5] (1918a) 'The Taboo of Virginity', S.E., Vol. 11, p. 204.

Case (1911) Freud refers to the man's feminine wish to be a woman submitting to intercourse.[1]

In 1913 Freud returns to the question of the confusion of the terms 'masculine' and 'feminine' with the qualities of 'activity' and 'passivity' and says that these latter qualities are determined not by the instincts themselves but by their aims. 'Infantile sexuality exhibits two other characteristics which are of importance from a biological point of view. It turns out to be put together from a number of component instincts which seem to be attached to certain regions of the body ('erotogenic zones') and some of which emerge from the beginning in pairs of opposites—instincts with an active and a passive aim.'[2]

'In spite of all our efforts to prevent biological terminology and considerations from dominating psycho-analytic work, we cannot avoid using them even in our descriptions of the phenomena that we study. We cannot help regarding the term "instinct" as a concept on the frontier between the spheres of psychology and biology. We speak, too, of "masculine" and "feminine" mental attributes and impulses, although, strictly speaking, the differences between the sexes can lay claim to no special psychical characterization. What we speak of in ordinary life as "masculine" or "feminine" reduces itself from the point of view of psychology to the qualities of "activity" and "passivity"—that is, to qualities determined not by the instincts themselves but by their aims. The regular association of these "active" and "passive" instincts in mental life reflects the bisexuality of individuals, which is among the clinical postulates of psychoanalysis'.[3]

In 1915, in 'Instincts and their Vicissitudes', Freud considers the question of instincts with active and passive aims in detail. He comments that 'Every instinct is a piece of activity; if we speak loosely of passive instincts, we can only mean instincts whose *aim* is passive.'[4] He also states that 'Reversal of an instinct into its opposite resolves on closer examination into two different processes; a change from activity to passivity, and a reversal of its content . . .

[1] (1911c) 'Psycho-Analytic Notes on an Autobiographical Account of a Case of Paranoia (Dementia Paranoides)', S.E., Vol. 12, p. 32.
[2] (1913j) 'The Claims of Psycho-Analysis to Scientific Interest', S.E., Vol. 13, p. 181.
[3] ibid., p. 182.
[4] (1915c) 'Instincts and their Vicissitudes', S.E., Vol. 14, p. 122.

'Examples of the first process are met with in the two pairs of opposites: sadism-masochism and scopophilia-exhibitionism. The reversal affects only the *aims* of the instincts. The active aim (to torture, to look at) is replaced by the passive aim (to be tortured, to be looked at). Reversal of *content* is found in the single instance of the transformation of love into hate.'[1] Freud comments that both aspects may be satisfied simultaneously, e.g., masochism is actually sadism turned round upon the subject's own body, and he continues: 'The essence of the process is thus the change of the *object*, while the aim remains unchanged. We cannot fail to notice, however, that in these examples the turning round upon the subject's self and the transformation from activity to passivity converge or coincide.'[2] In other words: the active-aim is to torture, then to torture oneself instead of the object, hence to be tortured— the instinct now has a passive aim. (At this point Freud doubted the existence of a primary masochism; a view which he reversed later in 'The Economic Problem of Masochism' (1924)—See also Concept on Masochism.)

Freud states that with regard to sadism and scopophilia 'it should be remarked that their transformation by a reversal from activity to passivity and by a turning round upon the subject never in fact involves the whole quota of the instinctual impulse. The earlier active direction of the instinct persists to some degree side by side with its later passive direction'.[3] (It is interesting that Freud here described this co-existence as 'ambivalence').[4]

He also comments that the first stage is one where the person's own body is the object of the scopophilic instinct, and must therefore be classed under narcissism; that the active aim is directed towards someone else's body and hence involves object-cathexis, while the passive aim holds fast to the narcissistic object—the person's own body. Thus the term 'passive scopophilic instinct' seems to refer only to the first developmental phase of autoerotism where the scopophilic instinct finds satisfaction on the subject's own body. 'We have become accustomed to call the early phase of the development of the ego, during which its sexual instincts find autoerotic satisfaction, "narcissism", without at once entering on any discussion of the relation between autoerotism and narcissism. It follows that the preliminary stage of the scopophilic

[1] ibid., p. 127.
[2] ibid., p. 127.
[3] ibid., p. 130.
[4] ibid., p. 131 and n.2.

ACTIVITY—PASSIVITY; MASCULINITY—FEMININITY

instinct, in which the subject's own body is the object of the scopophilia, must be classed under narcissism, and that we must
describe it as a narcissistic formation. The active scopophilic
instinct develops from this, by leaving narcissism behind. The
passive scopophilic instinct, on the contrary, holds fast to the
narcissistic object. Similarly, the transformation of sadism into
masochism implies a return to the narcissistic object. And in both
these cases [i.e. in passive scopophilia and masochism] the narcissistic *subject* is, through identification, replaced by another,
extraneous ego. If we take into account our constructed preliminary narcissistic stage of sadism, we shall be approaching a more
general realization—namely, that the instinctual vicissitudes which
consist in the instinct's being turned round upon the subject's own
ego and undergoing reversal from activity to passivity are dependent
on the narcissistic organization of the ego and bear the stamp of
that phase. They perhaps correspond to the attempts at defence
which at higher stages of the development of the ego are effected
by other means.'[1]

Freud said that he had only discussed the vicissitudes of sadism
and scopophilia because insufficient was known about the other
'ambivalent' sexual instincts, but he further suggests that these
first two instincts have a special significance in that they have great
need for an object in order to attain satisfaction, whereas other
instincts may be autoerotic, i.e. 'their object is negligible in comparison with the *organ* which is their source, and as a rule coincides
with that organ'. Freud quotes 'a plausible suggestion of Federn
(1913) and Jekels (1913)', that, 'the form and function of the organ
determine the activity or passivity of the instinctual aim'.[2]

In connection with the antithesis 'loving—being loved', Freud
says this 'corresponds exactly to the transformation from activity
to passivity and may be traced to an underlying situation in the same
way as . . . the scopophilic instinct. This situation is that of
loving oneself, which we regard as the characteristic feature of
narcissism. Then, according as the object or the subject is replaced
by an extraneous one, what results is the active aim of loving or
the passive one of being loved—the latter remaining near to
narcissism.'[3] 'The antithesis active-passive must not be confused
with the antithesis ego-subject—external world-object. The re-

[1] ibid., p. 131 f.   [2] ibid., p. 132 f.
[3] ibid., p. 133.

135

lation of the ego to the external world is passive in so far as it receives stimuli from it and active when it reacts to these ... the ego-subject is passive in respect of external stimuli but active through its own instincts. The antithesis active-passive coalesces later with the antithesis masculine-feminine, which, until this has taken place, has no psychological meaning. The coupling of activity with masculinity and of passivity with femininity meets us, indeed, as a biological fact; but it is by no means so invariably complete and exclusive as we are inclined to assume.'[1] (Freud discusses this point at greater length in a footnote which he added to the *Three Essays* in 1915.)[2]

Freud concludes this section: 'We may sum up by saying that the essential feature in the vicissitudes undergone by instincts lies in *the subjection of the instinctual impulses to the influences of three great polarities that dominate mental life*. Of these three polarities we might describe that of activity-passivity as the *biological*, that of ego-external world as the *real*, and finally that of pleasure-unpleasure as the *economic* polarity.'[3]

Slightly earlier (1914), when criticizing Adler's concept of 'The Masculine Protest', Freud comments that, 'Children have to begin with, no idea of the distinction between the sexes'; they start with the assumption that the penis is possessed by both sexes.[4]

In the paper 'On Narcissism' (1914) there is a detailed exposition of the development of object choice. This starts from the point when the child has two sexual objects—himself and his mother. Later he may make either a narcissistic or an anaclictic object-choice. 'Complete object-love of the attachment type is, properly speaking, characteristic of the male. It displays the marked sexual overvaluation which is doubtless derived from the child's original narcissism and thus corresponds to a transference of that narcissism to the sexual object. ... A different course is followed in the type of female most frequently met with. ... [Puberty] seems to bring about an intensification of the original narcissism, and this is unfavourable to the development of a true object choice

[1] ibid., p. 134.
[2] [1915] (1905d) *Three Essays on The Theory of Sexuality*, S.E., Vol. 7, p. 219, n.1.
[3] (1915c) 'Instincts and their Vicissitudes', S.E., Vol. 14, p. 140.
[4] (1914d) 'On the History of the Psycho-Analytic Movement', S.E., Vol. 14, p. 55.

136

with its accompanying sexual overvaluation. . . . Nor does their [women's] need lie in the direction of loving, but *of* being loved.'[1] However, 'In the child which they bear, a part of their own body confronts them like an extraneous object, to which, starting out from their narcissism, they can then give complete object-love. There are other women, again, who do not have to wait for a child in order to take the step in development from (secondary) narcissism to object-love. Before puberty they feel masculine and develop some way along masculine lines; after this trend has been cut short on their reaching female maturity, they still retain the capacity of longing for a masculine ideal.'[2]

In 1916–17, Freud wrote a series of *Introductory Lectures*, in one of which he summarized the early phases of sexual organization. Referring to the pre-genital organization, when the sadistic and anal instincts are most prominent he states: 'The contrast between "masculine" and "feminine" plays no part here as yet. Its place is taken by the contrast between "active" and "passive". . . . What appears to us as masculine in the activities of this phase, when we look at it from the point of view of the genital phase, turns out to be the expression of an instinct for mastery which easily passes over into cruelty. Trends with a passive aim are attached to the erotogenic zone of the anal orifice. . . . The instincts for looking and for gaining knowledge [the scopophilic and epistemophilic instincts] are powerfully at work. . . . The component instincts of this phase are not without objects, but those objects do not necessarily converge into a single object.'[3]

Further clinical material is given in the case history of the Wolfman, which shows the contrast between an early childhood stage of active sadistic fantasies and behaviour and the later adult passive, masochistic fantasies; this is linked with a contrast between the boy's first making a female object choice, and, after being rejected by her, seeking another sexual object, i.e. his father, but with a passive aim. The effect of external events which forced him into a passive role (e.g. seduction by his elder sister, observation of parental intercourse) is also traced.[4] This case history also contains a summary of the patient's psychopathology linking the

[1] (1914c) 'On Narcissism: an Introduction', S.E., Vol. 14, p. 88 f.
[2] ibid., p. 89 f.
[3] (1916–17) *Introductory Lectures on Psycho-Analysis*, S.E., Vol. 16, p. 327.
[4] (1918b[1914]) 'From the History of an Infantile Neurosis', S.E., Vol. 17, p. 26 f., 109 (cf. also ibid., p. 64, 79, 84, 101 f., 110–12 and 117 f.).

early wavering between activity and passivity with the adolescent struggle for masculinity, and shows that the narcissistic component was decisive in forming and maintaining his homosexual attitude.[1]

In another paper, Freud traces the vicissitudes of the woman's repressed wish to possess a penis. He shows that it may form neurotic symptoms, or it may have been transformed into the wish for a baby, or into the wish for a man—which by determining the object choice enables a pact of narcissistic masculinity to serve the female sexual function, i.e. to be changed into femininity.[2]

In a further paper, the differences and similarities between sadistic and masochistic fantasies in girls and boys are discussed: 'It must not be forgotten that when a boy's incestuous fantasy is transformed into the corresponding masochistic one, one more reversal has to take place than in the case of a girl, namely the substitution of passivity for activity; and this additional degree of distortion may save the fantasy from having to remain unconscious as a result of repression. In this way the sense of guilt would be satisfied by regression instead of by repression. In the female cases the sense of guilt, in itself perhaps more exacting, could be appeased only by a combination of the two.'[3] In the same paper Freud states: 'We are justified in assuming that no great change is effected by the *repression* of the original unconscious fantasy. Whatever is repressed from consciousness or replaced in it by something else remains intact and potentially operative in the unconscious. The effect of *regression* to an earlier stage of the sexual organization is quite another matter . . . the state of things changes in the unconscious as well. Thus in both sexes the masochistic fantasy of being beaten by the father, though not the passive fantasy of being loved by him, lives on in the unconscious after repression has taken place.'[4]

In 'A Case of Homosexuality in a Woman' (1920) Freud differentiated between the question of object choice on the one hand and of the sexual characteristics and sexual attitudes of the subject on the other: 'a man with predominantly male [social] characteristics and also masculine in his erotic life [instinctual aims] may

[1] ibid., p. 118.
[2] (1917c) 'On Transformations of Instinct as Exemplified in Anal Erotism', S.E., Vol. 17, p. 129 f.
[3] (1919e) 'A Child is Being Beaten', S.E., Vol. 17, p. 190.
[4] ibid., p. 199.

still be inverted in respect to his object, loving only men instead of women. A man in whose character feminine attributes obviously predominate, who may, indeed, behave in love like a woman might be expected, from this feminine attitude, to choose a man for his love-object; but he may nevertheless be heterosexual, and show no more inversion in respect to his object than an average normal man. The same is true of women; here also mental sexual character and object-choice do not necessarily coincide. . . . [Homosexuality] is instead a question of three sets of characteristics, namely:

Physical sexual characters—(physical hermaphroditism)
Mental sexual characters—(masculine or feminine attitude)
Kind of object-choice.'[1]

In his paper on the infantile genital organization (1923), Freud elaborated and gave a very clear summary of his views on sexual polarity. 'A first antithesis is introduced with the choice of object, which, of course, presupposes a subject and an object. At the stage of the pregenital sadistic-anal organization, there is as yet no question of male and female; the antithesis between *active* and *passive* is the dominant one. At the following stage of infantile genital organization . . . *maleness* exists, but not femaleness. The antithesis here is between having *a male genital* and being *castrated*. It is not until development has reached its completion at puberty that the sexual polarity coincides with *male* and *female*. Maleness combines [the factors of] subject, activity and possession of the penis; femaleness takes over [those of] object and passivity. The vagina is now valued as a place of shelter for the penis; it enters into the heritage of the womb.'[2]

In 'The Dissolution of the Oedipus Complex' (1924), Freud shows that the Oedipus complex offers the child 'two possibilities of satisfaction, an active and a passive one'. The boy can put himself either in father's or mother's place; both involve castration —either as a punishment, or as a feminine identification. Therefore the boy allies with his narcissistic interest in his penis against the libidinal cathexis of his parental objects—the boy's ego turns away from the Oedipus complex.[3]

[1] (1920a) 'The Psychogenesis of a Case of Female Homosexuality', S.E., Vol. 18, p. 170.
[2] (1923e) 'The Infantile Genital Organization of the Libido', S.E., Vol. 19, p. 145.
[3] (1924d) 'The Dissolution of the Oedipus Complex', S.E., Vol. 19, p. 176.

In another paper, Freud states that the boy's wanting to take his mother's place as the love object of his father, in the Oedipal situation, is described as the feminine attitude.[1] Discussing female development in the same paper, Freud comments that in the phallic phase, soon after the appearance of penis envy, the girl develops strong impulses *against* masturbation. He considers these impulses to be due to a narcissistic sense of humiliation (the clitoris being so inferior to the penis), and that they form a fore-runner to the wave of repression at puberty, which removes a large part of the girl's masculine sexuality.[2] In discussing the girl's Oedipal situation, Freud says:

'She gives up her wish for a penis and puts in place of it a wish for a child: and *with that purpose in view* she takes her father as a love-object. Her mother becomes the object of her jealousy. . . . When the girl's attachment to her father comes to grief later on . . . it may give place to an identification with him and the girl may thus return to her masculinity complex and perhaps remain fixated in it.' Freud then comments on the paradox that the castration complex destroys the Oedipus complex in boys, but in girls it makes possible and leads up to the Oedipus complex, and says, 'This contradiction is cleared up if we reflect that the castration complex always operates in the sense implied in its subject-matter: it inhibits and limits masculinity and encourages femininity.' The difference between male and female sexual development at this stage corresponds to the difference between a castration that has been carried out and one that has merely been threatened.[3] Freud then goes on to discuss the differences in superego formation in girls and boys; this is linked with the full shattering of the Oedipal complex in boys but does not happen to the same extent in girls.

In *Inhibitions, Symptoms and Anxiety* (1926) Freud gives clinical material illustrating the factors underlying a passive sexual attitude; he compares two cases (Little Hans and the Wolfman) to show the differences in degree of the underlying instinctual regression and the differences in the nature of the instinctual wishes defended against in the phobic symptoms.[4]

---

[1] (1925j) 'Some Psychological Consequences of the Anatomical Distinction between the Sexes', S.E., Vol. 19, p. 250.
[2] ibid., p. 255.   [3] ibid., p. 256 f.
[4] (1926d) *Inhibitions, Symptoms and Anxiety*, S.E., Vol. 20, pp. 105–8, p. 124.

In *Civilization and its Discontents* (1930), Freud restates his views on bisexuality; 'We are accustomed to say that every human being displays both male and female instinctual impulses, needs and attributes', and after pointing out that we should not too readily equate activity with maleness and passivity with femaleness, he says: 'if we assume it as a fact that each individual seeks to satisfy both male and female wishes in his sexual life, we are prepared for the possibility that those [two sets of] demands are not fulfilled by the same object, and that they interfere with each other unless they can be kept apart and each impulse guided into a particular channel that is suited to it. Another difficulty arises from the circumstance that there is so often associated with the erotic relationship, over and above its own sadistic components, a quota of plain inclination to aggression'.[1]

In 'Female Sexuality' (1931), there is a long discussion of the *active* element in the little girl's attitude towards her mother and in femininity in general. Freud mentions the child's early tendency to repeat actively that which it has experienced passively, whether the experience was pleasant or unpleasant. He mentions that the extent of this swingover from passivity to activity varies a great deal from child to child, and says that a child's behaviour in this respect may enable us to draw conclusions as to the relative strength of the masculinity and femininity that it will exhibit in its sexuality. He points out that what finds expression in a girl's playing with dolls is not true femininity but an active repetition of a passive experience.[2] The transformations of the little girl's aggressive oral and sadistic wishes are mentioned, and the emergence of the girl's wish to impregnate her mother. Freud also outlines the three paths which diverge from the point when the little girl discovers her organic inferiority of clitoris versus penis—(*a*) the one which leads to a cessation of her whole sexual life, (*b*) the one which leads to a defiant over-emphasis of her masculinity, and (*c*) the first steps towards definitive femininity.[3]

In 'Dostoevsky and Parricide' (1928), Freud had amplified his views on the boy's development, particularly in regard to the aggressive component. He showed that a boy's relation to his father is an ambivalent one, and that the trends of hate and tenderness

---

[1] (1930a) *Civilization and its Discontents*, S.E., Vol. 21, p. 106 n.
[2] (1931b) 'Female Sexuality', S.E., Vol. 21, p. 236 f.
[3] ibid., p. 232 and pp. 237–9.

THE LIBIDO THEORY

both combine to produce a masculine identification with the father.[1] He also refers to superego formation: 'If the father was hard, violent and cruel, the superego takes over those attributes from him and, in the relations between the ego and it, the passivity which was supposed to have been repressed is re-established. The superego has become sadistic, and the ego becomes masochistic—that is to say, at bottom passive in a feminine way.'[2]

In the *New Introductory Lectures* (1933) Freud recapitulates but also comprehensively draws together all the aspects of female sexuality which had hitherto been mentioned separately in his earlier papers.[3] Freud comments on the fact that where the woman's object choice does not meet with any serious internal or external obstacles, it is often made according to the narcissistic ideal of the man whom the girl would have liked to be.[4] He also refers to the two levels underlying the girl's identification with her mother—the 'affectionate' pre-Oedipal attachment and the Oedipal hostility, he adds that the phase of the tender pre-Oedipal attachment is the decisive one for her acquisitions of those characteristics which are necessary for her later femininity to be successful.[5]

In 'Analysis Terminable and Interminable' (1937), Freud mentions two prominent analytic themes (the wish for a penis in women, and the struggle against passivity in men) which are very troublesome to analyse. 'The two corresponding themes are in the female, an *envy for the penis*—a positive striving to possess a male genital—and, in the male, a struggle against his passive or feminine attitude to another male. What is common to the two themes was singled out at an early date by psychoanalytic nomenclature as an attitude towards the castration complex. Subsequently Alfred Adler brought the term masculine protest into current use. It fits the case of males perfectly; but I think that, from the start, repudiation of femininity would have been the correct description of this remarkable feature in the psychical life of human beings.

This 'factor . . . cannot, by its very nature, occupy the same position in both sexes. In males the striving to be masculine is

[1] (1928b) 'Dostoevsky and Parricide', S.E., Vol. 21, p. 183 f.
[2] ibid., p. 185.
[3] (1933a) *New Introductory Lectures on Psycho-Analysis*, S.E., Vol. 22, pp. 114–16, 117 f., 120, 126, 128–31.
[4] ibid., p. 132.   [5] ibid., p. 134.

142

completely ego-syntonic from the first; the passive attitude, since it presupposes an acceptance of castration, is energetically repressed, and often its presence is only indicated by excessive overcompensations. In females, too, the striving to be masculine is ego-syntonic at a certain period—namely in the phallic phase, before the development to femininity has set in. But it then succumbs to the momentous process of repression whose outcome . . . determines the fortunes of a woman's femininity. A great deal depends on whether a sufficient amount of her masculinity complex escapes repression and exercises a permanent influence on her character. Normally, large portions of the complex are transformed and contribute to the construction of her femininity: the appeased wish for a penis is destined to be converted into a wish for a baby and for a husband, who possesses a penis. It is strange, however, how often we find that the wish for masculinity has been retained in the unconscious and, from out of its state of repression, exercises a disturbing influence.

'As will be seen from what I have said, in both cases it is the attitude proper to the opposite sex which has succumbed to repression.'[1]

At the end of this section, Freud adds a footnote emphasizing what he did *not* mean by the terms active-passive:

'We must not be misled by the term "masculine protest" into supposing that what the man is repudiating is his passive attitude (as such)—what might be called the social aspect of femininity. Such a view is contradicted by an observation that is easily verifiable—namely that such men often display a masochistic attitude— a state that amounts to bondage—towards women. What they reject is not passivity in general, but passivity towards a male. In other words, the "masculine protest" is in fact nothing else than castration anxiety.'[2]

Finally, in *An Outline of Psycho-Analysis* (1938), Freud says, when discussing the effects of the castration complex in boys and girls:

'The results of the threat of castration are multifarious and incalculable; they affect the whole of a boy's relations with his father and mother and subsequently with men and women in general. As a rule the child's masculinity is unable to stand up to this first

[1] (1937c) 'Analysis Terminable and Interminable', S.E., Vol. 23, p. 250 f.
[2] ibid., p. 252

143

shock. In order to preserve his sexual organ he renounces the possession of his mother more or less completely; his sexual life often remains permanently encumbered by the prohibition. If a strong feminine component, as we call it, is present in him, its strength is increased by this intimidation of his masculinity. He falls into a passive attitude to his father, such as he attributes to his mother. It is true that as a result of the threat he has given up masturbation, but not the activities of his imagination accompanying it. On the contrary, since these are now the only form of sexual satisfaction remaining to him, he indulges in them more than before and in these fantasies, though he still continues to identify himself with his father, he also does so, simultaneously and perhaps predominantly with his mother. Derivatives and modified products of these early masturbatory fantasies usually make their way into his later ego and play a part in the formation of his character. Apart from this encouragement of his femininity, fear and hatred of his father gain greatly in intensity. The boy's masculinity withdraws, as it were, into a defiant attitude towards his father, which will dominate his later behaviour in human society in a compulsive fashion. A residue of his erotic fixation to his mother is often left in the form of an excessive dependence on her, and this persists as a kind of bondage to women. He no longer ventures to love his mother, but he cannot risk not being loved by her, for in that case he would be in danger of being betrayed by her to his father and handed over to castration.'[1]

A few pages later Freud continues:

'The effects of the castration complex in little girls are more uniform and less profound. A female child has, of course, no need to fear the loss of a penis; she must, however, react to the fact of not having received one. . . . If during the phallic phase she tries to get pleasure like a boy by the manual stimulation of her genitals, it often happens that she fails to obtain sufficient satisfaction and extends her judgement of inferiority from her stunted penis to her whole self. . . .

'If a little girl adheres to her first wish—to grow into a boy—in extreme cases she will end as a manifest homosexual, and otherwise she will exhibit markedly masculine traits in the conduct of her later life, will choose a masculine vocation, and so on. The other path leads by way of abandoning the mother she has loved:

[1] (1940a [1938]) *An Outline of Psycho-Analysis*, S.E., Vol. 23, p. 190 f.

the daughter, under the influence of her envy for the penis, cannot forgive her mother for having sent her into the world so insufficiently equipped. In her resentment over this she gives up her mother and puts someone else in her place as the object of love—her father. If one has lost a love-object, the most obvious reaction is to identify oneself with it, to replace it from within, as it were, by identification. This mechanism now comes to the little girl's help. Identification with her mother can take the place of attachment to her mother . . . she tries to take her mother's place with her father, and begins to hate the mother she used to love, and from two motives: from jealousy as well as from mortification over the penis she has been denied. Her new relation to her father may start by having as its content a wish to have his penis at her disposal, but it culminates in another wish—to have a baby from him as a gift. . . .

'It does little harm to a woman if she remains in her feminine Oedipus attitude. (The term "Electra complex" has been proposed for it). She will in that case choose her husband for his paternal characteristics and be ready to recognize his authority. Her longing to possess a penis, which is in fact unappeasable, may find satisfaction if she can succeed in completing her love for the organ by extending it to the bearer of the organ, just as happened earlier when she progressed from her mother's breast to her mother as a whole person.'[1]

[1] ibid., p. 193 f.

SCOPOPHILIA

SEE CONCEPTS: *Component Instincts, Exhibitionism*

Definition

The scopophilic instinct is one among many component instincts which, when integrated under the primacy of the genital zone, constitute the sexual instinct as known in mature adult sexuality.

It is a component with an active sexual aim—that is the aim to look at. It is always found with *Exhibitionism* and always precedes it; i.e. the active component of looking always precedes the *passive* component of being looked at.[1]

Manifestations of Scopophilia

Scopophilia plays a role in normal sexual life. Under certain conditions it plays a role in perversions such as voyeurism, fetishism, homosexuality.

As will be described below it is a significant factor in the obsessional neuroses.

Historical Survey

In 1905. Freud pointed out that normal pleasure in looking becomes a perversion if it is restricted solely to the genitals; if it is connected with the overriding of disgust (as in the case of *voyeurs*); and if it supplants the normal sexual aim instead of being preparatory to it. The force which opposes scopophilia, but which may be overridden by it, is shame.[2]

In the same paper he notes that 'Whenever we find in the unconscious an instinct of this sort which is capable of being paired off with an opposite one, this second instinct will regularly be found in operation as well. Every active perversion is thus accompanied by its passive counterpart: anyone who is an exhibitionist in his unconscious is at the same time a *voyeur*'.[3]

In 1909: Freud illustrated the role of scopophilia in the analysis

---

[1] (1905d) *Three Essays on the Theory of Sexuality*, S.E., Vol. 7, p. 167.
[2] ibid., p. 157.   [3] ibid., p. 167.

of Little Hans.[1] In his analysis of the Ratman he drew attention to the fact that certain symptoms in obsessional neurosis arise from a process of repression and displacement to which the scopophilic instinct has been subjected.[2]

In the same paper Freud showed how the histories of obsessional patients invariably revealed 'an early development and premature repression of the sexual instinct of looking and knowing' [the scopophilic and the epistemopholic instinct].[3]

Scopophilia is the main component in children's sexual curiosity which often has the quality of an instinctual drive. It may become sublimated in a real interest in research or its repressions may block any intellectual interest depending upon what experiences have become associated with this instinctive curiosity.[4]

In 1910: Freud's paper, 'The Psychoanalytic View of Psychogenic Disturbance of Vision' describes the outcome of these repressions. If scopophilia has been repressed, inhibitions of looking come to the fore. The sexual component instinct of scopophilia is, like its passive counterpart, exhibitionism, subject to numerous restrictions and transformations. Under normal conditions both instincts, which are allowed free expression in early childhood, are subjected to a considerable measure of repression and sublimation later on. In some cases, however, these instincts are inhibited and transformed to a very much greater degree while, at the same time, they carry on a continual struggle against the forces of repression. While five years before, in the *Three Essays,* he had described the eye as corresponding to an erotogenic zone,[5] in the present paper he expanded his earlier views on the role of the eye in scopophilia and on the effects of repressing these component sexual instincts.

He now stated that: 'the eyes perceive not only alterations in the external world which are important for the preservation of life, but also characteristics of objects which lead to their being chosen as objects of love—their charms. The saying that it is not easy for anyone to serve two masters is thus confirmed. The closer the relation into which an organ with a dual function of this kind

[1](1909b) 'Analysis of a Phobia in a Five-Year-Old Boy', S.E., Vol. 10, pp. 106 f. and 127.
[2] (1909d) 'Notes upon a Case of Obsessional Neurosis', S.E., Vol. 10, p. 162.
[3] ibid., pp. 244-7.
[4] (1907c) 'The Sexual Enlightenment of Children', S.E., Vol. 9, pp. 131-9,
[5] (1905d) *Three Essays on the Theory of Sexuality,* S.E., Vol. 7, p. 169.

THE LIBIDO THEORY

enters with *one* of the major instincts, the more it withholds itself from the other. This principle is bound to lead to pathological consequences if the two fundamental instincts are disunited and if the ego maintains a repression of the sexual component instinct concerned.'[1]

If the scopophilic impulse has become too strong (or directed towards forbidden objects) then a conflict results in the subject's instinctual life. The sexual pleasure of looking 'has drawn upon itself defensive action by the ego-instincts in consequence of its excessive demands, so that the ideas in which its desires are expressed succumb to repression and are prevented from becoming conscious; in that case there will be a general disturbance of the relation of the eye and of the act of seeing to the ego and consciousness. The ego will have lost its dominance over the organ, which will now be wholly at the disposal of the repressed sexual instinct. ... The loss of conscious dominance over the organ is the detrimental substitute for the repression which had miscarried and was only made possible at that price.'[2]

Here Freud includes the idea of talion punishment, 'Because you sought to misuse your organ of sight for the evil sensual pleasures, it is fitting that you should not see anything at all any more'.[3]

In *Three Essays on the Theory of Sexuality* Freud assumed that certain component instincts, such as scopophilia, exhibitionism and cruelty, involved other people as sexual objects. He continued to say that in a sense they appear independently of the erotogenic zones and do not enter into intimate relations with genital (sexual was the word used in 1905 and 1910 editions at this point) life until later, but are already to be observed in childhood as independent impulses, distinct, in the first instance, from erotogenic sexual activity.[4]

This formulation was modified in 1915 ('Instincts and their Vicissitudes') on the basis of the introduction of the concept of narcissism (1914). Freud now stated: 'For the beginning of its activity the scopophilic instinct is autoerotic; it has indeed an object, but that object is part of the subject's own body. It is only

[1] (1910i) 'The Psycho-Analytic View of Psychogenic Disturbances of Vision', S.E., Vol. 11, p. 216.
[2] ibid., p. 216.
[3] ibid., p. 217.
[4] (1905d) *Three Essays on the Theory of Sexuality*, S.E., Vol. 7, p. 192.

later that the instinct is led, by a process of comparison, to exchange this object for an analogous part of someone else's body.'[1]

Freud suggested in 'Instincts and Their Vicissitudes' that all instincts have a pressure, an aim, an object and a source; and further that an instinct may undergo the vicissitudes of (a) reversal into its opposite, (b) turning around upon the subject's own self, (c) repression and (d) sublimation.

(a) *Reversal*: Scopophilia and exhibitionism are a pair of opposites. The reversal affects only the aims of each. The active aim —to look at—is replaced by the passive aim—to be looked at. Reversal of content occurs *only* in the transformation of love into hate.

(b) *Turning around upon the subject's self:* For the beginning of its activity the scopophilic instinct is autoerotic. It necessarily must precede exhibitionism because, in the first instance, the infant is the subject and the object at the same time. He is the subject in so far as he is looking at, and he is the object in so far as he is being looked at.

Only subsequently is looking 'an activity directed towards an extraneous object'. This object is then given up and the scopophilic instinct is turned towards a part of the subject's own body. A new passive aim is therefore set up—the aim to be looked at. In the final stage a new subject is introduced (to whom one displays oneself in order to be looked at by him).[2]

The exhibitionist shares in the enjoyment of (the sight of) his own exposure. While the object is changed, the aim remains the same. Freud pointed out that the turning around on the subject's self, and the transformation from activity to passivity, coincide.[3]

(c) *Repression:* Freud showed that the repression of the scopophilic instinct may result in the formation of symptoms. He wrote in 1905: ' . . . my researches into the early years of normal people, as well as of neurotic patients, force me to the conclusion that scopophilia can also appear in children as a spontaneous manifestation. Small children whose attention has once been drawn— as a rule by masturbation—to their own genitals usually take the further step without help from outside and develop a lively interest in the genitals of their playmates. Since opportunities for satisfying

[1] (1915e) 'The Unconscious', S.E., Vol. 14, p. 130.
[2] ibid., p. 129.
[3] ibid., p. 126 f.

curiosity of this kind usually occur only in the course of satisfying the two kinds of need for excretion, children of this kind turn into voyeurs, eager spectators of the processes of micturition and defecation. When repression of these inclinations sets in, the desire to see other people's genitals (whether of their own or the opposite sex) persists as a tormenting compulsion, which in some cases of neurosis later affords the strongest motive force for the formation of symptoms.'[1]

(d) *Sublimation:* Freud wrote in 1905 that seeing is an activity 'ultimately derived from touching' and he went on: 'Visual impressions remain the most frequent pathway along which libidinal excitation is aroused; indeed, natural selection counts upon the accessibility of this pathway . . . when it encourages the development of beauty in the sexual object. The progressive concealment of the body which goes along with civilization keeps sexual curiosity awake. This curiosity seeks to complete the sexual object by revealing its hidden parts. It can, however, be diverted ("sublimated") in the direction of art, if its interest can be shifted away the genitals on to the shape of the body as a whole. It is usual for most normal people to linger to some extent over the intermediate sexual aim of a looking that has a sexual tinge to it; indeed, this offers them a possibility of directing some proportion of their libido on to higher artistic aims. On the other hand this pleasure in looking (scopophilia) becomes a perversion. . . .'[2]

In his paper on *Leonardo da Vinci and a Memory of His Childhood* Freud observed further: 'Leonardo emerges from the obscurity of his boyhood as an artist, a painter and a sculptor, owing to a specific talent which may have been reinforced by the precocious awakening in the first years of childhood of his scopophilic instinct.'[3]

Clinical Applications

In the same paper he drew attention to the clinical significance of the scopophilic instinct: 'Before the child comes under the dominance of the castration-complex—at a time when he still holds women at their full value—he begins to display an intense desire to look, as an erotic instinctual activity. He wants to see

---

[1] (1905d) *Three Essays on the Theory of Sexuality,* S.E., Vol. 7, p. 192.
[2] ibid., p. 156 f.
[3] (1910c) *Leonardo da Vinci and a Memory of His Childhood,* S.E., Vol. 11, p. 132

other people's genitals, at first in all probability to compare them with his own. The erotic attraction that comes from his mother soon culminates in a longing for her genital organ, which he takes to be a penis. With the discovery, which is not made till later, that women do not have a penis, this longing often turns into its opposite and gives place to a feeling of disgust which in the years of puberty can become the cause of psychical impotence, misogyny and permanent homosexuality. But the fixation on the object that was once strongly desired, the woman's penis, leaves indelible traces on the mental life of the child, who has pursued that portion of his infantile sexual researches with particular thoroughness. Fetishistic reverence for a woman's foot and shoe appears to take the foot merely as a substitutive symbol for the woman's penis which was once revered and later missed; without knowing it, *coupeurs de nattes* play the part of people who carry out an act of castration on the female genital organ.'[1]

Fetishism: In the *Three Essays on the Theory of Sexuality* Freud first described the significance of *fetishism*. He showed that the fetish was a substitute for an infantile sexual object and that the selection of the fetish object was influenced by a *coprophilic* smell attraction. Later he emphasized the fact that the fetish symbolized the penis and its presence relieved the castration fear of the male, a fear which was aroused by the sight of the female genital. 'Probably no human being is spared the fright of castration at the sight of a female genital,' he observed.[2]

Turning to specific manifestations, Freud wrote: 'In a number of cases of foot fetishism it has been possible to show that the scopophilic instinct, seeking to reach its object (originally the genitals) from underneath, was brought to a halt in its pathway by prohibition and repression. For that reason it became attached to a fetish in the form of a foot or shoe, the female genitals (in accordance with the expectations of childhood) being imagined as male ones.'[3]

Voyeurs and Exhibitionists: For voyeurs and exhibitionists the normal preparatory act becomes the abnormal sexual aim. They seek gratification in looking and touching or in watching the other person's most intimate doings. Such perverts may sometimes

---

[1] ibid., p. 96.
[2] (1927e) 'Fetishism', S.E., Vol. 21, p. 154.
[3] (1905d) *Three Essays on the Theory of Sexuality*, S.E., Vol. 7, p. 155.

expose parts of their own bodies in the vague expectation of achieving a reciprocal action on the part of the other.[1]

The genital organs are retained as object: 'not, however, on account of their sexual function but of other functions in which the genital plays a part either for anatomical reasons or because of its propinquity. We find from them that the excretory functions, which have been put aside as improper during the upbringing of children, retain the ability to attract the whole of sexual interest'.[2]

The Neurosis: Freud in 1905, called attention to the significance of the component instincts, which introduce new sexual aims, in the formation of symptoms in the psychoneuroses.[3]

He illustrated how in *obsessional neurosis* the excessive 'worry' and 'brooding' are the expressions of an exaggerated sexualization of acts which normally are only preparatory to sexual satisfaction. These introductory acts involve the desire to look, to touch, and to explore.[4]

Analytic Technique: Freud pointed out that the scopophilic patient, entering analysis, may regard lying on the couch as a hardship and may rebel against it.[5]

---

[1] (1916–17) *Introductory Lectures on Psycho-Analysis*, S.E., Vol. 16, p. 306.
[2] ibid., p. 305.
[3] (1905d) *Three Essays on the Theory of Sexuality*, S.E., Vol. 7, p. 166.
[4] (1916–17) *Introductory Lectures on Psycho-Analysis*, S.E., Vol. 16, p. 309.
[5] (1913c) 'On Beginning the Treatment (Further Recommendations on the Technique of Psycho-Analysis, I)', S.E., Vol. 12, p. 134.

EXHIBITIONISM

SEE CONCEPT: *Scopophilia, Component Instincts*

Definition
Exhibitionism is the term used by Freud to refer to a component of the sexual instinct. He characterized it as having a passive aim, namely that of being looked at. In this sense it is the counterpart of the scopophilic components whose aim is to look at.[1]

Freud noted: 'Whenever we find ... an instinct of this sort which is capable of being paired off with an opposite one, this second instinct will regularly be found in operation as well ... anyone who is an exhibitionist in his unconscious is at the same time a *voyeur* ...'[2]

Exhibitionism plays a role in normal sexual life. Under certain conditions it can become a perversion.[3]

Historical Survey
Freud's study of the role of exhibitionism underwent compara- tively little change from the time he first drew attention to its importance in 1900. His main statements on the subject are to be found in *The Interpretation of Dreams* (1900), the *Three Essays on The Theory of Sexuality* (1905), 'The Psycho-Analytic View of Psychogenic Disturbance of Vision' (1910) and in 'Instincts and their Vicissitudes' (1915).

In 1900
Freud noted that nakedness induces no shame in children—indeed that most children derive pleasure from their exposure. 'When we look back at this unashamed period of childhood it seems to us a Paradise;' he wrote, 'and Paradise itself is no more than a group fantasy of the childhood of the individual. That is why mankind were naked in Paradise and were without shame in one another's presence; till a moment arrived when shame and anxiety awoke,

---

[1] (1915c) 'Instincts and their Vicissitudes', S.E., Vol. 14, p. 127.
[2] (1905d) *Three Essays on the Theory of Sexuality*, S.E., Vol. 7, p. 167.
[3] ibid., p. 157.

expulsion followed, and sexual life and the tasks of cultural activity began. But we can regain this Paradise every night in our dreams.' He argued that these earliest childhood impressions strive to achieve reproduction and their repetition (in dreams) constitutes the fulfilment of a wish. 'Thus dreams of being naked are dreams of exhibiting', he concluded.[1]

He maintains that various factors will remain constant in a typically exhibitionist dream. The dreamer will appear, not as he was as a child but as he currently is, inadequately clothed. There will be spectators, not those who peopled the infantile scenes of exhibiting but invariably strangers with indeterminate features. These onlookers neither object to, nor even notice, the acutely embarrassing lack of clothing (which represents the wish fulfilment). The dreamer, nevertheless, is overcome by feelings of intense shame and embarrassment. Yet a powerful inhibition bars him from moving, or changing his distressing situation of nakedness. The sense of distress is a reaction against the act of exhibiting which, itself, has defied the 'censorship' processes.[2]

In 1905

Freud in *Three Essays on the Theory of Sexuality* said 'seeing' derives ultimately from 'looking' and 'visual impressions remain the most frequent pathway along which libidinal excitation is aroused'. Most normal people 'linger . . . over the intermediate sexual aim of a looking that has a sexual tinge to it'. And he set forth three conditions in which scopophilia or exhibitionism could become a perversion:

(*a*) If it is restricted solely to the genitals.

(*b*) If it is connected with the overriding of disgust (as in voyeurs or people who look on at excretory functions).

(*c*) If it supplants, instead of preparing for, the normal aim. Exhibitionists will display their own genitals to obtain a reciprocal view of the genitals of another.

'The force which opposes this scopophilia, but which may be overridden by it, is shame,' Freud observed.[3]

When shame prevents the initial satisfaction derived by a child from exposure, it produces a curiosity to see other people's

---

[1] (1900a) *The Interpretation of Dreams*, S.E., Vol. 4, p. 244 f.
[2] ibid., pp. 242–6.
[3] (1905d) *Three Essays on the Theory of Sexuality*, S.E., Vol. 7, p. 156 f.

genitals. Since children can satisfy this curiosity mainly by observing micturition and defecation they could develop into voyeurs.

In 1910
Freud's paper on 'The Psycho-analytic View of Psychogenic Disturbance of Vision' expanded his earlier work on the role of the eye in scopophilia and exhibitionism and on the effects of repressing these component sexual instincts. He had, five years before, described the eye as corresponding to an erotogenic zone.[1] Now he wrote: '... the eyes perceive not only alterations in the external world which are important for the preservation of life, but also characteristics of objects which lead to their being chosen as objects of love—their charms. The saying that it is not easy for anyone to serve two masters is thus confirmed. The closer the relation into which an organ with a dual function of this kind enters with *one* of the major instincts, the more it withholds itself from the other. This principle is bound to lead to pathological consequences if the two fundamental instincts are disunited and if the ego maintains a repression of the sexual component instinct concerned.' If the scopophilic impulses has become too strong (or directed towards forbidden objects) then a conflict results in the subject's instinctual life. The sexual pleasure of looking 'has drawn upon itself defensive action by the ego-instincts in consequence of its excessive demands, so that the ideas in which its desires are expressed succumb to repression and are prevented from becoming conscious; in that case there will be a general disturbance of the relation of the eye and the act of seeing to the ego and consciousness. The ego will have lost its dominance over the organ, which will now be wholly at the disposal of the repressed sexual instinct. ... The loss of conscious dominance over the organ is the detrimental substitute for the repression which had miscarried and was only made possible at that price.'[2]

In 1915
According to Freud's theory all instincts have a pressure, an aim, an object and a source. Furthermore they may undergo the vicissitudes of (*a*) reversal into the opposite, (*b*) turning around

[1] ibid., p. 169.
[2] (1910i) 'The Psycho-Analytic View of Psychogenic Disturbance of Vision', S.E., Vol. 11, p. 216.

upon the subject's own self, (c) repression and (d) sublimation.

(a) Reversal. Exhibitionism and scopophilia are a pair of opposites. The reversal affects only the aims of each. The active aim—to look at—is replaced by the passive aim—to be looked at.

(b) Turning around upon the subject's self. The exhibitionist shares in the enjoyment of (the sight of) his exposure. While the object is changed, the aim remains the same. Freud pointed out that the turning around on the subject's self, and the transformation from activity to passivity, coincide.[1]

At first the scopophilic instinct (preceding exhibitionism) is autoerotic. 'It has indeed an object but that object is part of the subject's own body.' Only later, through a process of comparison, the instinct is led to exchange this object for an analogous part of someone else's body. Both scopophilia and exhibitionism, therefore, share the common precursor in the sexual aim of looking at oneself.

Freud postulated three stages in the change of object in this pair of opposites.

(i) Looking as an activity directed towards an extraneous object.

(ii) Giving up of the object and turning of the scopophilic instinct towards a part of the subject's own body. When this occurs there is a transformation to passivity and the new aim of being looked at is set up.

(iii) Introduction of a new subject to whom one displays oneself in order to be looked at by him.[2]

The active scopophilia instinct (looking at an extraneous object) leaves narcissism behind whereas exhibitionism holds fast to the narcissistic object. Due to its origin the erogenous pleasure in exhibitionism is always connected with an increase in self-esteem, anticipated or actually gained through the fact that others look at the subject.[3]

(c) Repression. ' . . . if in the course of development some of the components which are of excessive strength in the disposition are submitted to the process of repression . . . they are prevented by psychical obstruction from attaining their aim and are diverted into numerous other channels till they find their way to expression as symptoms'.[4]

[1] (1915c) 'Repression', S.E., Vol. 14, pp. 122–7.
[2] ibid., p. 129 f.   [3] ibid., p. 132.
[4] (1905d) Three Essays on the Theory of Sexuality, S.E., Vol. 7, p. 237 f.

(*d*) Sublimation. If the exhibitionist instinct is sublimated there may result an 'impulsion to artistic and theatrical display'.[1] In a 1920 footnote to the *Three Essays on the Theory of Sexuality*, Freud drew attention to the part exhibitionism plays in the castration complex. Exhibitionism in men may remain fixed to the genitals where it plays a role in sexual fore-pleasure. The compulsion to exhibit is a means of 'constantly insisting upon the integrity of the subject's own (male) genitals and it reiterates his infantile satisfaction at the absence of a penis in those of women'.[2]

The erect male organ also has apotropaic effect. To exhibit the penis means 'I am not afraid of you. I defy you. I have a penis.'[3]

Normal Manifestations of Exhibitionism

The libido for looking 'is present in everyone in two forms, active and passive, male and female; and, according to the preponderance of the sexual character, one form or the other predominates.'[4]

The most commonplace manifestation is to be found in children who derive satisfaction from exposing sexual parts of their bodies. In adults exhibitionism can take other forms, ranging from women who wear attention-getting clothes to the humorist who wants to display his cleverness by the persistent telling of jokes.[5] Each of these manifestations could be equated with exhibitionism in the sexual field. Similarly Freud likened a person's tendency towards 'smut' with the tendency towards sexual exposure. Wooing a woman with words or ideas aims essentially at exciting her and so awaking her inclination to passive exhibitionism.[6]

Clinical Manifestations of Exhibitionism

'In the early history of neurotics an important part is played by exposure to children of the opposite sex; in paranoia delusions of being observed while dressing and undressing are to be traced back to experiences of this kind; while among persons who have remained at the stage of perversion there is one class in which this infantile impulse has reached the pitch of a symptom, the class of "exhibitionists".'[7]

[1] (1910a) 'Five Lectures on Psycho-Analysis', S.E., Vol. 11, p. 44.
[2] (1905d) *Three Essays on the Theory of Sexuality*, S.E., Vol. 7, p. 157.
[3] (1940c [1922]) 'Medusa's Head', S.E., Vol. 18, p. 274.
[4] (1905c) *Jokes and their Relation to the Unconscious*, S.E., Vol. 8, p. 98.
[5] ibid., pp. 98–101 and 143.   [6] ibid., p. 98 f.
[7] (1900a) *The Interpretation of Dreams*, S.E., Vol. 4, p. 244, cf. also (1905d) *Three Essays on the Theory of Sexuality, S.E., Vol. 7.*

PERVERSION

Definition

A perversion is a form of adult sexual activity which deviates from normal adult sexuality by virtue of the gratification being exclusively attained either through inappropriate objects and/or derived through the satisfaction of instinctual aims other than the normal aim of sexual union which is in the service of the reproductive function. Freud's metapsychological formulations of these deviations suggest that the ego's sanctioning of the regression to pre-genital modes of satisfaction represents in many cases a defence against the great anxiety engendered by genital sexuality.

Brief History

Freud's published notions regarding the nature of perversions date back to 1895. From then until 1905 a number of references to perversions are to be found, but these lack any systematic treatment; these references do contain the germs of his later thinking regarding the nature and aetiology of these sexual aberrations. It was in 1905, in the *Three Essays*, that Freud offered his most extended analysis of the perversions; these formulations remain as the basic core of his theory of perversions. This analysis was part of a systematic evaluation of the nature of the sexual instinct and its components—and indeed of the very nature of human sexuality; while many of the statements about perversions were aimed largely to demonstrate that their roots lay in childhood sexuality, it would seem that Freud's formulations of the perversions were reciprocally dependent on the formulations regarding the sexual instinct. The subject of perversions received added insights with Freud's later formulations regarding phase development—particularly the phallic phase, the related issues of castration anxiety and the Oedipus complex, the libidinal position of narcissism, ego and superego development, and the death instinct.

Pre-1905 Formulation

Few definitions of perversion are to be found in Freud's writings before 1901. One such reference occurs in a letter to Fliess

158

'... zones which no longer produce a release of sexuality in normal and mature human beings must be the regions of the anus and of the mouth and throat. ... In animals these sexual zones retain their power. ... where they do so in human beings, the result is perversion'[1] Early in his writing Freud raised the question of choice of disorder (neurosis *v.* perversion): '... how does it come about that analogous conditions (sexual seduction in childhood) sometimes give rise to perversion or simple immorality instead of to a neurosis?'[2] This was to be a subject for life-long inquiry. In the latter letter he spoke of the necessary preconditions for the development of neurosis, the lack of which would predispose one to perversion: '... shame and morality are the repressing forces. ... Where there is no shame (as in male persons) or no morality (as in the lower classes of society), there too, infantile sexual stimulation will not lead to repression, nor consequently to neurosis'.[3] Implicit in this formulation is the notion that 'perverse impulses' (pregenital sexuality) characterize early human life and are normally abandoned by virtue of education and developing repressive forces.

One early hypothesis as to whether a seduced child would develop a neurosis or perversion was based on the notion of bisexuality. He said: 'In order to explain why the outcome is sometimes perversion and sometimes neurosis, I will avail myself of the universal bisexuality of human beings. In a purely male being there would be a surplus of masculine release at the two sexual boundaries, consequently pleasure would be released; in a purely female being there would be surplus of unpleasurable substance (after an initial surplus of pleasure). ... This explains the preference of true females for the defensive neurosis'.[4] This highly 'organic' hypothesis, developed at a time when influenced by Fliess' theory of bisexuality, was never referred to again although the more psychological concept of bisexuality was to remain a basic tenet; the question of the differential susceptibility to neurosis or perversion on the part of males and females was still occupying him in 1905. (It is not clear what Freud meant by 'sexual boundaries'. This is probably a construct which Freud used in connection with the hypothecation of 'sexual substances'—the opera-

[1] (1950a [1887–1902]) *The Origins of Psychoanalysis*, London, Imago, 1954, Letter No. 75, 14.11.1897.
[2] ibid., p. 147. Draft K. 1.1.1896.
[3] ibid., p. 147.   [4] ibid., p. 179. Letter 52, 6.12.1896.

tion of which (i.e. their flow, discharge, accumulation, etc.) was seen as explaining the origin of such disorders as anxiety neurosis and neurasthenia).

Some of Freud's early statements regarding the relation of hysteria to perversion were to be maintained in his later writings. The essential point was that hysteria represented a defence against the expression of strong perverse impulses. In Letter No. 52 (6.12.1896) he said: '. . . hysteria is in fact not repudiated *sexuality* but rather repudiated perversions'.[1] He also said in 1897, 'I am toying with the idea that in the perversions, of which hysteria is the negative, we may have the remnants of a primitive sexual cult . . .'[2] The first part of this statement was to remain a basic dictum while the second part was abandoned as a hypothesis.

In 'Fragment of an Analysis of a Case of Hysteria', written in and published in 1905, Freud bridged the gap between the perversions and 'normal' sexuality. He spoke of perversions as '. . . a development of germs all of which are contained in the undifferentiated sexual disposition of the child . . . and which, by being suppressed or by being diverted to higher asexual aims— by being sublimated—are destined to provide the energy for a great number of our cultural achievements'.[3] Instead of perversions representing alien and degenerate forms of sexual behaviour, which was the popularly accepted notion of the time, Freud spoke of them as 'inhibitions of development: when, therefore, anyone has become a *gross* and manifest pervert, it would be more correct to say that he has *remained* one, for he exhibits a certain stage of inhibited development'.[4] Also at this time Freud made an attempt at classifying the perversions which was to foreshadow his elaboration of these deviations in terms of aim and object. He said that 'the sexual perversions are instances in which the sexual function has extended its limits in respect either to the part of the body concerned or to the sexual object chosen'.[5] He reiterated his notions regarding the relationship between perversions and psychoneurosis, saying: 'All psychoneurotics are persons with strongly marked perverse tendencies, which have become repressed in the course of their development and have become unconscious. Consequently their unconscious fantasies

[1] ibid., p. 180.   [2] ibid., p. 189. Letter 57, 24.1.1897.
[3] (1905e[1901]) 'Fragment of an Analysis of a Case of Hysteria', S.E., Vol. 7, p. 50.   [4] ibid., p.50.   [5] ibid., p. 50.

show precisely the same content as the documentarily recorded *actions* of perverts. . . . Psychoneuroses, are, so to speak, the *negative* of perversions.'[1]

1905 Formulation

In the *Three Essays* Freud enlarged upon the nature of perversions in terms of component sexual instincts. He classified the perversions as: '. . . sexual activities which either (a) extend, in an anatomical sense, beyond the regions of the body that are designed for sexual union, or (b) linger over the intermediate relations to the sexual object which should normally be traversed rapidly on the path towards the final sexual aim.'[2] These behaviours were seen in terms of 'fixations'—either to pre-genital erotogenic zones or to one or more of the component instincts. However, he did not consider these fixations to be truly pathological unless they fulfilled the basic criterion of perversions—that of 'exclusiveness'. He said: 'In the majority of instances the pathological character in a perversion is found to lie not in the *content* of a new sexual aim but in its relation to the normal. If a perversion, instead of appearing merely alongside the normal sexual aim and object, and only when circumstances are unfavourable to them and favourable to *it*—if, instead of this, it ousts them completely and takes their place in *all* circumstances—if, in short, a perversion has the characteristics of exclusiveness and fixation—then we shall usually be justified in regarding it as a pathological symptom.'[3] In contrast to these latter cases and in the attempt to show that (a) sexual development rarely proceeds without individual variations in the strength of a given component instinct or pre-genital zone and (b) that such 'perverse' sexual behaviours in the 'normal' adult function as 'fore-pleasures' preparatory to the aim of genital union, he said: 'Everyday experience has shown that most of these extensions, or at any rate the less severe of them, are constituents which are rarely absent from the sexual life of healthy people. . . .'[4]

He pointed to such behaviours as kissing, touching, looking, etc., as normal preparatory acts to sexual intercourse; yet, these behaviours can become independent of this final aim and be ends

[1] ibid., p. 50 f.
[2] (1905d) *Three Essays on the Theory of Sexuality*, S.E., Vol. 7, p. 150
[3] ibid., p. 161.   [4] ibid., p. 160.

in themselves, achieving for the person complete sexual satisfaction.

In discussing the question of the innateness of perversions Freud pointed to childhood sexuality as indicating that the disposition to perversion ' . . . is something innate in *everyone*, though as a disposition it may vary in its intensity and may be increased by the influences of actual life'.[1] Furthermore, he said: ' . . . the extraordinarily wide dissemination of the perversions forces us to suppose that the disposition to perversions is itself of no great rarity but must form a part of what passes as the normal constitution'.[2] He noted: ' . . . under the influence of seduction children can become polymorphously perverse, and can be led into all possible kinds of sexual irregularities. This shows that an aptitude for them is innately present in their disposition'.[3]

In discussing the factors that contribute to fore-pleasures being in themselves an aim, he said: 'Experience has shown that the precondition for this damaging event is that the erotogenic zone concerned or the corresponding component instinct shall already during childhood have contributed an unusual amount of pleasure. If further factors then come into play, tending to bring about a fixation, a compulsion may easily arise in later life which resists incorporation of this particular fore-pleasure into a new context. Such is in fact the mechanism of many perversions, which consist in a lingering over the preparatory acts of the sexual process.'[4]

Once again Freud pointed to certain mental forces which act as 'resistances' ('psychical inhibitions') such as shame and disgust, which ordinarily come to the fore in the course of development and prevent the expression of 'perverse impulses in normal adults'. Indeed, the lack of such restraining inner forces in early childhood and in the perversions provided a clearer view of the very nature of the sexual instinct. He said: 'If such perversions admit of analysis, that is, if they can be taken to pieces, then they must be of a composite nature. This gives us a hint that perhaps the sexual instinct itself may be no simple thing, but put together from components which have come apart again in the perversions'.[5] In view of these apparent dissociations, Freud was led to say: 'The perversions were thus seen to be on the one hand inhibitions, and on the other hand, dissociations, of normal development'.[6]

Freud held to the view that 'neurosis is the negative of per-

[1] ibid., p. 171.   [2] ibid., p. 171.   [3] ibid., p. 191.
[4] ibid., p. 162.   [5] ibid., p. 162.   [6] ibid., p. 231.

versions', first voiced back in 1897. He spoke of psychoneurosis as
being a 'negative perversion' in that the neurotic symptoms reflect
the defence ('repression') against strong perverse impulses. In
speaking to the question of a constitutional predisposition to
neurosis, Freud said: ' . . . what appears to be the strong tendency
(though, it is true, a negative one) of psychoneurotics to perversion may be colaterally determined, and must, in any case be
collaterally intensified. The fact is that we must put sexual repression as an internal factor alongside such external factors as
limitation of freedom, inaccessibility of a normal sexual object,
the dangers of the normal sexual, etc., etc., which bring about
perversions in persons who might otherwise have remained
normal'.[1] Freud here emphasized the interaction of constitutional
and accidental factors in the development of the 'tendency to
perversion' in psychoneurosis.[2] (It should be kept in mind that at
this point he was using the term 'constitution' largely to refer to
the strength or weakness of particular component instincts.) Freud
supported his view of the 'essential connections' between psychoneurosis and perversion by pointing to his empirical observation
of the frequency of occurrence of these disorders within particular
families; the male members were seen as developing perversions
('positive perverts') while the females 'true to the tendency of
their sex to repression', developed hysterias—a 'negative perversion'.[3] He also emphasized that a constitutional weakness of the
genital zone may foster the development of perversion: 'For if the
genital zone is weak, this combination which is required to take
place at puberty, is bound to fail, and the strongest of the other
components of sexuality will continue its activity as a perversion'.
The origin of fetishism was then seen as a special case[4] of this
hypothesized genital weakness.[5]

In those perversions involving looking and being looked at, and
in sadism and masochism, Freud made special note of the fact that
the sexual aim occurred in two forms—an active and a passive one.
In speaking of sadism and masochism, which he termed 'the most
common and most significant of all the perversions',[6] he said:
' . . . certain among the impulses to perversion occur regularly as

[1] ibid., p. 170. [2] ibid., p. 170 f.
[3] ibid., p. 236. [4] ibid., p. 237.
[5] (1905e[1901]) 'Fragment of an Analysis of a Case of Hysteria', S.E., Vol. 7,
p. 53.
[6] (1905d) *Three Essays on the Theory of Sexuality*, S.E., Vol. 7, p. 157.

pairs of opposites.... We should be inclined to connect the simultaneous presence of these opposites with the opposing masculinity and femininity which are combined in bisexuality'.[1] He stressed the operation of both the active and passive forms of the perversion in the Unconscious. With regard to perversions, he said, ' . . . in the actual symptoms one or the other of the opposing tendencies plays the predominant part'.[2]

Post-1905 Additions and Modifications
Beginning in 1908, with the publication of 'Civilized Sexual Morality and Modern Nervous Illness', Freud's writings reflect increasing attention to the *objects* of the sexual instinct in the perversions. At this time he spoke of two different kinds of sexual aberrations: ' . . . *perverts*, in whom an infantile fixation to a preliminary sexual aim has prevented the primacy of the reproductive function from being established, and the *homosexuals* or *inverts*, in whom, in a manner that is not yet quite understood, the sexual aim has been deflected away from the opposite sex'.[3] In 1909, in 'Analysis of a Phobia in a Five-year-Old Boy' (Little Hans), Freud characterized homosexuals as: ' . . . persons who, owing to the erotogenic importance of their own genitals, cannot do without a similar feature in their sexual object. In the course of their development from autoerotism to object-love, they have remained at a point of fixation between the two'.[4] This point was more fully developed and extended in his 1914 paper, 'On Narcissism'; at this point he did not distinguish so sharply the disorders of perversion from those of homosexuality. He said: 'We have discovered, especially clearly in people whose libidinal development has suffered some disturbance, such as perverts and homosexuals, that in their later choice of love-objects they have taken as a model not their mother but their own selves . . . a type of object-choice which must be termed "narcissistic".'[5] In a 1915 addition to the *Three Essays*, when discussing the 'castration complex', Freud said of boys, 'The substitutes for this penis which they feel is missing in women play a great part in determining the form taken by many perversions'.[6]

[1] ibid., p. 160.   [2] ibid., p. 167.
[3] (1908d) ' "Civilized" Sexual Ethics and Modern Nervous Illness', S.E., Vol. 9, p. 189.
[4] (1909b) 'Analysis of a Phobia in a Five-Year-Old Boy', S.E., Vol. 10, p. 109.
[5] (1914c) 'On Narcissism: an Introduction', S.E., Vol. 14, p. 88.
[6] (1905d) *Three Essays on the Theory of Sexuality*, S.E., Vol. 7, p. 195.

In the 1915 edition of the *Three Essays*, Freud posited clearly that not only was fixation involved in the perversions but also regression, i.e. that these persons had proceeded to higher levels of libidinal development but were unable to maintain them. In speaking of the role of *'repression'* in psychoneurotics, he said: 'This does not apply only to the "negative" tendencies to perversion which appear in neuroses but equally to the "positive", properly so-called, perversions. Thus these latter are to be derived not merely from a fixation of infantile tendencies but also a regression to those tendencies as a result of other channels of the sexual current being blocked'.[1] This positing of the role of repression as a factor in bringing about regression was an important amplification, since previously the development of perversions was seen as reflecting the absence of repressive forces. The factor of repression leading to regression was not noted in the previous year in 'On Narcissism'; referring to the repressive function of the 'ego-ideal'—instead of to the previous references to shame, disgust, etc., he said: 'The ego-ideal has imposed severe conditions upon the satisfaction of libido through objects; for it causes some of them to be rejected by means of its censor—as being incompatible. Where no such ideal has been formed, the sexual trend in question makes its appearance unchanged in the personality in the form of a perversion'.[2] In an addition to the *Three Essays* in 1915, alongside the factor of repression, he again cited the role of 'genital weakness' in the regression to pre-genital sexuality: ' . . . one often finds that at puberty a normal sexual current begins to operate at first, but that as a result of its internal weakness, it breaks down in the face of the first external obstacles and is then replaced by regression to the perverse fixation'.[3]

In the *Introductory Lectures* (1916–17) Freud summarized his views on perversions in an extended exposition. He affirmed again the two major criteria for judging sexual activities as perversions: where 'the purpose of reproduction is put on one side' and the 'exclusiveness with which these deviations are carried out'.[4] These deviations were seen as affecting either the sexual aim or the sexual object. (Homosexuality was now placed in the class of perversions rather than as an independent disorder.) A second

[1] ibid., p. 232.
[2] (1914c) 'On Narcissism: an Introduction', S.E., Vol. 14, p. 100.
[3] (1905d) *Three Essays on the Theory of Sexuality*, S.E., Vol. 7, 237, n. 1.
[4] (1916–17) *Introductory Lectures on Psycho-Analysis*, S.E., Vol. 16, p. 322.

distinction was also made: 'alongside of those who seek their sexual satisfaction in reality are those who are content merely to *imagine* that satisfaction, who need no real object at all, but can replace it by their fantasies'.[1] He reiterated the notion that 'some perverse trait or other is seldom absent from the sexual life of normal people'.[2] What distinguished these manifestations from those seen in perversions was that they did not lead to orgasm and emission in the normal adult. Another feature, related to 'Exclusiveness', was seen as the 'centred' focus on one dominant pregenital component impulse which determined the one aim of sexual satisfaction. This characteristic differentiated perversions from infantile sexuality where ' . . . component instincts have equal rights, each of them goes its own way to obtaining pleasure';[3] normal adult sexuality also shows the dominance and organization by a ruling component impulse, but one which aims at ultimate genital union. In contrast to the perversions' centred sexual expression, Freud pointed to cases of 'infantilism': ' . . . cases of perverse sexuality which have a much greater resemblance to the infantile kind, since in them numerous component instincts have put through (or, more correctly, have persisted in) their aims independently of one another. It is better in such cases to speak of infantilism in sexual life rather than of a perversion.'[4]

The concept of 'adhesiveness of the libido' ('the tenacity with which the libido holds to particular trends and objects') was seen as a 'determining' but not solely sufficient factor in the development of perversions. (Such fixations were also to be seen in neurotics and normal people.) The origin of such fixations was seen as an unknown, although Freud said that ' . . . a very early impression of an abnormal instinctual trend or choice of object was quite often found, to which the subject's libido remained attached all through his life'.[5] He stressed the interaction of accidental factors and constitutional predisposition in the formation of such fixations and noted that accidental factors often served to trigger off the 'innate predisposition' of certain of the component instincts coming to expression. In regard to the sexual constitution, he hypothesized the influence of phylogenetic inheritance ('ancestral experiences') but did not attempt to link this factor to development of perversions.

[1] ibid., p. 306.   [2] ibid., p. 322.   [3] ibid., p. 323.
[4] ibid., p. 323.   [5] ibid., p. 348.

When regression to these fixation points occurred, the ego was seen as either condoning them or finding them unacceptable. 'If these regressions rouse no objection from the ego, no neurosis will come about either; and the libido will arrive at some real, even though no longer normal, satisfaction. But if the ego . . . does not agree with these regressions, conflict will follow.'[1] Freud also said, 'A regression of the libido without repression would never produce a neurosis but would lead to a perversion'.[2] Freud was here not negating his 1915 citing of the operation of repression in perversion. Repression was seen as *occasioning* the regression to the perverse fixation; but it did not operate, as it did with psychoneurotics, to reject the expression of pregenital impulses once the regression had occurred.

In 1919, Freud saw the Oedipus complex as a key factor in the development of perversions. In 'A Child is Being Beaten' he said: ' . . . the constitutional reinforcement or premature growth of a single sexual component is not shaken, indeed; but it is seen not to comprise the whole truth. . . . [Perversion] first comes into prominence in the sphere of this complex [Oedipus], and after the complex has broken down it remains over, often quite by itself, the inheritor of the charge of libido from that complex and weighed down by the sense of guilt that was attached to it'.[3] The constitutional predisposition for this particular reaction is maintained: 'The abnormal sexual constitution . . . has shown its strength by forcing the Oedipus complex into a particular direction, and by compelling it to leave an unusual residue behind'.[4] He said that childhood perversions could either continue in adulthood or remain in the background of a normal sexual life. However, he said of the former: ' . . . we find often enough with these perverts that they too made an attempt at developing normal sexual activity, usually at the age of puberty; but their attempt had not enough force in it and was abandoned in the face of obstacles which inevitably arise, whereupon they fell back upon their infantile fixation once and for all'.[5] In a 1920 footnote to the *Three Essays* Freud again cited repression as a factor in this regression: ' . . . perversions are a residue of development towards

[1] ibid., p. 359.   [2] ibid., p. 344.
[3] (1919e) 'A Child is Being Beaten', S.E., Vol. 17, p. 192.
[4] ibid., p. 192.
[5] ibid., p. 192.

the Oedipus complex and . . . after the repression of that complex
the components of the sexual instinct which are strongest in the
disposition of the individual concerned emerge once more'.[1]

In 1923, in considering the differential reactions of the ego in
conflict situations, in this case with regard to whether the outcome
is neurosis or psychosis, Freud noted that economic considerations
of the strength of conflicting forces were of foremost importance.
(This emphasis was long existent in his earlier works, particularly
in his discussion of complemental series in the 1915 edition of the
Three Essays and in the *Introductory Lectures*). Following this
discussion he introduced the idea that the ego in conflict with its
'ruling agencies' might allow for the expression of perversions in
the aim of maintaining its own existence. He said: ' . . . it will be
possible for the ego to avoid a rupture in any direction by deform-
ing itself, by submitting to encroachments on its own unity and even
by effecting a cleavage or division of itself. In this way the in-
consistencies, eccentricities and follies of men would appear in a
similar light to their sexual perversions, through the acceptance
of which they spare themselves repressions'.[2] Freud came to call
this development a 'split in the ego'.

A major mechanism in this process is that of '*disavowal*'. This
was first described in 1910, in Freud's study of *Leonardo da
Vinci*, when he commented that certain fetishes are symbolic
equivalents for the 'missing penis' in women. This was described
more fully in 'Fetishism' (1927, S.E. 21) where 'disavowal' was
seen as representing a defence against an unacceptable aspect of
reality, in this case, a penisless woman. He distinguished between
disavowal and repression as defences against ideas and affects
respectively. The fetish itself was seen as representing the 'missing
penis' which is on the one hand accepted as a reality and on the
other hand is denied. Freud came back to the concepts of 'split in
the ego' and 'disavowal' in 1938 in *An Outline of Psycho-Analysis*.
He then said: ' . . . the ego often enough finds itself in the position
of fending off some demand from the external world which it feels
distressing and . . . this is effected by means of a *disavowal* of the
perceptions. . . . The disavowal is always supplemented by an
acknowledgement; two contrary and independent attitudes always
arise and result in the situation of there being a splitting of the

[1] (1905d) *Three Essays on the Theory of Sexuality*, S.E., Vol. 7, p. 162, n.3.
[2] (1924b) 'Neurosis and Psychosis', S.E., Vol. 19, p. 152 f.

ego'.[1] After pointing out that this phenomenon in adults was not limited to psychoses, but also to 'other states more like the neuroses', he spoke of the fetishist 'not recognizing the fact that females have no penis—a fact which is extremely undesirable to him since it is a proof of the possibility of his being castrated himself'.[2] (One is reminded that Freud had earlier described homosexuals as having reacted intensely to the 'recognition' that women had no penis; his analysis of this reaction at that time was in terms of the 'castration complex' and the narcissistic threat of this knowledge.)

Another hypothesis as to the development of perversions, this time in reference to the perversions of sadism and masochism, was that of the *defusion* of Eros and the Death Instinct. In 1923, in *The Ego and the Id*, Freud said: 'The sadistic component of the sexual instinct would be a classical example of a serviceable instinctual fusion; and the sadism which has made itself independent as a perversion would be typical of a defusion, though not of one carried to extremes'.[3] (Freud's 1905 statement that perhaps perversions were an outcome of the dissociation of the sexual instinct, so that the component instincts 'came apart', as it were, should not be related too closely to this formulation of defusion which involves both the sexual *and* aggressive drives, cf. S.E. 7, p. 162.)

No further references to the hypothesis of instinctual defusion leading to perversions in sexual life are to be found. It should be noted, however, that sadism and masochism tended to be viewed independently of the other perversions. For example, in the 1905 edition of the *Three Essays* he characterized sadism and masochism as 'the most common and significant of all the perversions'.[4] In the 1915 edition he said, 'Sadism and masochism occupy a special position among the perversions since the contrast between activity and passivity which lies behind them is among the universal position among the perversions, since the contrast between ac-*Three Essays*, 1924, he said: ' . . . researches . . . have led me to assign a peculiar position, based upon the origin of instincts, to the

---

[1] (1940a[1938]) *An Outline of Psycho-Analysis*, S.E., Vol. 23, pp. 203–4.
[2] ibid., p. 202.
[3] (1923b) *The Ego and the Id*, S.E., Vol. 19, p. 41.
[4] (1905d) *Three Essays on the Theory of Sexuality*, S.E., Vol. 7, p. 157.
[5] ibid., p. 159.

pair of opposites constituted by sadism and masochism, and to place them outside the class of the remaining "perversions".' [1]

Some Clinical Considerations

In the course of his writings Freud occasionally commented on the social adaptation and treatability of perverts. In 1905, after describing some inverts as accepting their inversion while others 'rebel' against it and feel it as a pathological compulsion, he said, 'The fact of a person struggling in this way against a compulsion towards inversion may perhaps determine the possibility of his being influenced by suggestion (added 1910) or psychoanalysis'.[2] He noted wryly that it was difficult to assess the hereditary factors among perverts 'for they know how to avoid investigation'.[3] In 1905, he also noted that many homosexuals were ' . . . distinguished by specially high intellectual development and ethical culture'.[4] Again, in 1908, he spoke of homosexuals showing a 'special aptitude for cultural sublimation'; however, he added, 'More pronounced forms of the perversions and of homosexuality, especially if they are exclusive, do, it is true, make those subject to them socially useless and unhappy, so that it must be recognized that the cultural requirements . . . are a source of suffering for a certain proportion of mankind'.[5] Those whose sexual instinct was 'weak' he saw as capable of suppressing their impulses but noted that this suppression left them 'inwardly inhibited and outwardly paralyzed'.[6] In the *Introductory Lectures*, Freud again commented on the high intellectual and ethical attainments of many homosexuals, but he added the more sobering note that, ' . . . there are at least as many inferior and useless individuals among them as there are among those of a different sexual kind'.[7] In 1923, in one of his final statements regarding treatability, he listed the perversions as one of the disorders that was amenable to psychoanalytic treatment.[8] He had noted in 1915 that the perversions were accessible to treatment since, like neurotics, they showed features of fixation, repression, and regression.[9]

[1] ibid., p. 159.   [2] ibid., p. 137, n.1.
[3] ibid., p. 236.   [4] ibid., p. 139.
[5] (1908d) ' "Civilized" Sexual Ethics and Modern Nervous Illness', S.E., Vol. 9, p. 190.   [6] ibid., p. 190.
[7] (1916–17) *Introductory Lectures on Psycho-Analysis*, S.E., Vol. 16, p. 305.
[8] (1923a) 'Two Encyclopaedia Articles', S.E., Vol. 18, p. 250.
[9] [1915] (1905d) *Three Essays on the Theory of Sexuality*, S.E., Vol. 7, p. 232, n.1.

THE CASTRATION COMPLEX

SEE CONCEPTS: *The Phallic Phase, Oedipus Complex*
Dissolution of Oedipus Complex, Activity-Passivity,
Masculinity-Femininity

Introduction
Freud has defined the 'Castration Complex' as 'the reaction to the threats against the child aimed at putting a stop to his early sexual activities and attributed to his father'.[1] In his view the fear of castration has a phylogenetic basis and he suspected that in the primeval period castration was actually carried out by a 'jealous and cruel father' on growing boys and he considered that circumcision is a relic of this.[2]

Its significance *'can only be rightly appreciated if its origin in the phase of phallic primacy is also taken into account'*. It is concerned with 'those excitations and consequences which are bound up with the loss of the penis'.[3]

It is as important for girls as for boys, Freud wrote that 'we are justified in speaking of a castration complex in women as well. Both male and female children form a theory that women no less than men originally had a penis, but that they have lost it by castration'.[4] He also wrote that 'with their entry into the phallic phase the differences between the sexes are completely eclipsed by their agreements'.[5]

Early History of Term
In the *Interpretation of Dreams* there is what Strachey in his Introductions calls a 'single obscure' reference to the threat of castration. A fourteen-year-old boy who was referred for attacks of hysterical vomiting, headaches, etc., was told by Freud to shut his eyes and verbalize the pictures he saw. He saw a sickle. This emerged as

[1] (1916–17) *Introductory Lectures on Psycho-Analysis*, S.E., Vol. 16, p. 208.
[2] (1933a) *New Introductory Lectures on Psycho-Analysis*, S.E., Vol. 22, p. 86 f.
[3] (1923e) 'The Infantile Genital Organization of the Libido', S.E., Vol. 19, p. 144.
[4] [1920] (1905d) *Three Essays on the Theory of Sexuality*, S.E., Vol. 7, p. 195 n,
[5] (1933a) *New Introductory Lectures on Psycho-Analysis*, S.E., Vol. 22, p. 118.

related to the family situation and his father's recent marriage. The father was described as a hard and angry person who had been left by the boy's mother and the sickle was the one with which Zeus castrated his father in the myth. The boy now had the opportunity to repay 'the reproaches and threats which he had heard from his father long before because he had played with his genitals'.[1]

It was in 1908 in 'On the Sexual Theories of Children' that Freud first wrote of the child's notion of the possession of the penis by members of both sexes. Penis envy was mentioned for the first time explicitly and the 'castration complex' discussed.[2]

The first hints as to the fact of 'penis envy' in girls appears in a letter to Fliess on November 14, 1897, in which Freud wrote that 'The main distinction between the two sexes emerges at the period of puberty, when a non-neurotic distaste for sexuality overtakes girls and libido asserts its hold on men. For at that period a further sexual zone is partly or wholly extinguished in females, which persists in males. What I have in mind is the male genital zone, the region of the clitoris, in which during childhood sexual sensitivity seems to be concentrated in girls as well as boys'.[3]

In another context Freud wrote that: 'The two corresponding themes are, in the female, an *envy for the penis*—a positive striving to possess a male genital—and, in the male, a struggle against his passive or feminine attitude to another male. What is common to the two themes was singled out at an early date by psycho-analytic nomenclature as an attitude towards the castration complex.'[4]

In 'Little Hans' the term as such appears to have been used for the first time when the patient began to show 'a quite peculiarly lively interest in that portion of his body which he used to describe as his "widdler". Thus he once asked his mother this question:

'Hans: "Mummy, have you got a widdler too?"

. . . Meanwhile his interest in widdlers was by no means a purely theoretical one; as might have been expected, it also impelled him to *touch* his member. When he was three and a half his mother found him with his hand on his penis. She threatened

---

[1] (1900a) *The Interpretation of Dreams*, S.E., Vol. 5, p. 619.

[2] (1908c) 'On the Sexual Theories of Children', S.E., Vol. 9, p. 215 f.

[3] Freud, S., *The Origins of Psychoanalysis, Letters to Wilhelm Fliess*, London, Imago, p. 233.

[4] (1937c) 'Analysis Terminable and Interminable', S.E., Vol. 23, p. 250.

him in these words: "If you do that, I shall send for Dr A. to cut off your widdler. And then what'll you widdle with?"

'Hans: "With my bottom".

'He made this reply without having any sense of guilt as yet. But this was the occasion of his acquiring the "castration complex", the presence of which we are so often obliged to infer in analyzing neurotics, though they one and all struggle violently against recognizing it. There is much of importance to be said upon the significance of this element in the life of a child. The "castration complex" has left marked traces behind it in myths (and not only in Greek myths); in a passage in my *Interpretation of Dreams* (1900), and elsewhere, I have touched upon the part it plays.'

In a footnote added in 1923 Freud wrote: 'Since this was written, the study of the castration complex has been further developed in contributions to the subject by Lou Andreas-Salome (1960), F. Alexander (1922), and others. It has been urged that every time his mother's breast is withdrawn from a baby he is bound to feel it as castration (that is to say, as the loss of what he regards as an important part of his own body); that, further, he cannot fail to be similarly affected by the regular loss of his faeces; and, finally, that the act of birth itself (consisting as it does in the separation of the child from his mother, with whom he has hitherto been united) is the prototype of all castration. While recognizing all of these roots of the complex, I have nevertheless put forward the view that the term "castration complex" ought to be confined to those excitations and consequences which are bound up with the loss of the *penis*. Any one who, in analyzing adults, has become convinced of the invariable presence of the castration complex, will of course find difficulty in ascribing its origin to a chance threat—of a kind which is not, after all, of such universal occurrence; he will be driven to assume that children construct this danger for themselves out of the slightest hints, which will never be wanting.'[1]

The castration complex is closely linked to the Oedipus complex and as such was viewed by Freud as one of the main 'cornerstones of psychoanalysis'. The following quotation links the two complexes in the male sex at any rate, in terms of the fear of the father as castrator and the quotation further specifies the symbolic equation of castration and blindness. He wrote that 'the same part is played by the father alike in the Oedipus and the castration com-

---

[1] (1909b) 'Analysis of a Phobia in a Five-Year-Old Boy', S.E., Vol. 10, p. 8.

plexes—the part of a dreaded enemy to the sexual interests of childhood. The punishment which he threatens is castration, or its substitute, blinding'.[1]

Development of the castration complex in the boy
In the development of the small child the castration complex is preceded by the child's 'intense desire to look as an erotic instinctual activity. He wants to see other people's genitals, at first in all probability to compare them with his own. The erotic attraction that comes *from* his mother soon culminates in a longing for her genital organ, which he takes to be a penis. With the discovery, which is not made till later, that women do not have a penis, this longing often turns into its opposite and gives place to a feeling of disgust'.[2] 'The terror of Medusa is thus a terror of castration that is linked to the sight of something . . . [It] occurs when a boy, who has hitherto been unwilling to believe the threat of castration, catches sight of the female genitals, probably those of an adult, surrounded by hair and essentially those of his mother.'[3] The little boy concludes that girls have 'a penis as well, only it is still very small; it will grow later . . . [or] it was cut off. . . . Under the influences of this threat of castration he now sees the notion he has gained of the female genitals in a new light; henceforth he will tremble for his masculinity'.[4] With the castration complex he suffers 'the severest trauma of his young life'.[5] The 'narcissistic interest' in the penis[6] leads him to find 'that part of his body too valuable and too important . . . to believe that it could be missing in other people whom he feels he resembles so much'.[7] 'The boy enters the Oedipus phase; begins to manipulate his penis and simultaneously has fantasies of carrying out some sort of activity with it in relation to his mother, till, owing to the combined effect of a threat of castration and the sight of the absence of a

[1] (1912–13) *Totem and Taboo*, S.E., Vol. 13, p. 130.
[2] (1910c) *Leonardo da Vinci and a Memory of His Childhood*, S.E., Vol. 11, p. 96.
[3] (1940c[1922]) 'Medusa's Head', S.E., Vol. 18, p. 273.
[4] (1910c) *Leonardo da Vinci and a Memory of His Childhood*, S.E., Vol. 11, p. 95.
[5] (1940a[1938]) *An Outline of Psycho-Analysis*, S.E., Vol. 23, p. 190.
[6] (1925j) 'Some Psychological Consequences of the Anatomical Distinction between the Sexes', S.E., Vol. 19, p. 250.
[7] (1910c) *Leonardo da Vinci and a Memory of His Childhood*, S.E., Vol. 11, p. 95.

penis in females, he experiences the greatest trauma of his life and this introduces the period of latency with all its consequences'.[1]

The impact of the 'castration threat' on the child is greater when he reaches the phallic phase which implies a special cathexis of the penis. It is now that such threats become more meaningful. Freud refers to the heightened value attached to the penis and its excitations in the following quotation: 'The child, having been mainly dominated by excitations in the penis, will usually have obtained pleasure by stimulating it with his hand; he will have been detected in this by his parents or nurse and terrorized by the threat of having his penis cut off. The effect of this "threat of castration" is proportionate to the value set upon that organ and is quite extraordinarily deep and persistent. Legends and myths testify to the upheaval in the child's emotional life and to the horror which is linked with the castration complex.'[2]

He links this cathexis of the penis to the child's attempts at understanding adult sexuality when he says 'the penis certainly has a share, too, in these mysterious happenings; the excitation in it which accompanies all these activities of the child's thoughts bears witness to this. Attached to this excitation are impulsions which the child cannot account for—obscure urges to do something violent, to press in, to knock to pieces, to tear open a hole somewhere'.[3]

Elsewhere it is described as bringing about the dissolution of the Oedipus complex. 'But now his acceptance of the possibility of castration, his recognition that women were castrated, made an end of both possible ways of obtaining satisfaction from the Oedipus complex. For both of them entailed the loss of his penis— the masculine one as a resulting punishment and the feminine one as a precondition. If the satisfaction of love in the field of the Oedipus complex is to cost the child his penis, a conflict is bound to arise between his narcissistic interest in that part of his body and the libidinal cathexis of his parental objects. In this conflict the first of these forces normally triumphs: the child's ego turns away from the Oedipus complex.'[4]

---

[1] (1940a) *An Outline of Psycho-Analysis*, S.E., Vol. 23, p. 155.
[2] (1908c) 'On the Sexual Theories of Children', S.E., Vol. 9, p. 217.
[3] ibid., p. 218.
[4] (1924d) 'The Dissolution of the Oedipus Complex', S.E., Vol. 19, p. 176.

Development of the Castration Complex in the Boy

Thus, in boys, the castration complex was considered to bring about the destruction of the Oedipus complex. Freud wrote that certain elements in the prehistory of the Oedipus complex in boys remains unclear. He wrote 'We know that that period includes an identification of an affectionate sort with the boy's father, an identification which is still free from any sense of rivalry in regard to his mother. Another element of that stage is invariably, I believe, a masturbatory activity in connection with the genitals, the masturbation of early childhood, the more or less violent suppression of which by those in charge of the child sets the castration complex in action.'[1]

As indicated above before the emergence of the castration complex it is 'when a little boy first catches sight of a girl's genital region, [that] he begins by showing irresolution and lack of interest; he sees nothing or disavows what he has seen, he softens it down or looks about for expedients for bringing it in line with his expectations. It is not until later, when some threat of castration has obtained a hold upon him, that the observation becomes important to him: if he then recollects or repeats it, it arouses a terrible storm of emotion in him and forces him to believe in the reality of the threat which he has hitherto laughed at. This combination of circumstances leads to two reactions, which may become fixed and will in that case, whether separately or together or in conjunction with other factors, permanently determine the boy's relations to women: horror of the mutilated creature or triumphant contempt for her'.[2]

Elsewhere Freud stated: 'Later on he takes fright at the possibility thus presented to him; and any threats that may have been made to him earlier, because he took too intense an interest in his little organ, now produce a deferred effect. He comes under the sway of the castration complex, the form taken by which plays a great part in the construction of his character if he remains normal, in his neurosis if he falls ill, and in his resistances if he comes into analytic treatment.'[3]

Elsewhere the processes are summarized as follows: 'The results

[1] (1925j) 'Some Psychological Consequences of the Anatomical Distinction between the Sexes', S.E., Vol. 19, p. 250.
[2] ibid., p. 252.
[3] (1916–17) Introductory Lectures on Psycho-Analysis, S.E., Vol. 16, p. 317 f.

of the threat of castration are multifarious and incalculable; they affect the whole of a boy's relations with his father and mother and subsequently with men and women in general. As a rule the child's masculinity is unable to stand up against this first shock. In order to preserve his sexual organ he renounces the possession of his mother more or less completely; his sexual life often remains permanently encumbered by the prohibition. If a strong feminine component, as we call it, is present in him, its strength is increased by this intimidation of his masculinity. He falls into a passive attitude to his father, such as he attributes to his mother. It is true that as a result of the threat he has given up masturbation, but not the activities of his imagination accompanying it. On the contrary, since these are now the only form of sexual satisfaction remaining to him, he indulges in them more than before, and in these phantasies, though he still continues to identify himself with his father, he also does so, simultaneously and perhaps predominantly, with his mother. Derivatives and modified products of these early masturbation phantasies usually make their way into his later ego and play a part in the formation of his character. Apart from this encouragement of his femininity, fear and hatred of his father gain greatly in intensity. The boy's masculinity withdraws, as it were, into a defiant attitude towards his father, which will dominate his later behaviour in human society in a compulsive fashion. A residue of his erotic fixation to his mother is often left in the form of an excessive dependence on her, and this persists as a kind of bondage to women. He no longer ventures to love his mother, but he cannot risk not being loved by her, for in that case he would be in danger of being betrayed by her to his father and handed over to castration.'[1]

In discussing anxiety Freud referred to Little Hans' horse phobia and the Wolfman's wolf phobia and how these stemmed from fear of castration by the father.

'It was the fear of impending castration. "Little Hans" gave up his aggressiveness towards his father from fear of being castrated. His fear that a horse would bite him can, without any forcing, be given the full sense of a fear that a horse would bite off his genitals, would castrate him. But it was from fear of being castrated, too, that the little Russian relinquished his wish to be loved by his father, for he thought that a relation of that sort presupposed a

[1] (1940a) An Outline of Psycho Analysis, S.E., Vol. 23, p. 190 f.

sacrifice of his genitals—of the organ which distinguished him from a female. As we see, both forms of Oedipus complex, the normal, active form and the inverted one, came to grief through the castration complex. The Russian boy's anxiety-idea of being devoured by a wolf contained, it is true, no suggestion of castration, for the oral regression it had undergone had removed it too far from the phallic stage. But the analysis of his dream rendered further proof superfluous. It was a triumph of repression that the form in which his phobia was expressed should no longer have contained any allusion to castration.

'Here, then, is our unexpected finding: in both patients the motive force of the repression was fear of castration. The ideas contained in their anxiety—being bitten by a horse and being devoured by a wolf—were substitutes by distortion for the idea of being castrated by their father. This was the idea which had undergone repression. In the Russian boy the idea was an expression of a wish which was not able to subsist in the face of his masculine revolt; in "Little Hans" it was the expression of a reaction in him which had turned his aggressiveness into its opposite. But the *affect* of anxiety, which was the essence of the phobia, came, not from the process of repression, not from the libidinal cathexes of the repressed impulses, but from the repressing agency itself. The anxiety belonging to the animal phobias was an untransformed fear of castration. It was therefore a realistic fear, a fear of a danger which was actually impending or was judged to be a real one. It was anxiety which produced repression and not, as I formerly believed, repression which produced anxiety.

'It is no use denying the fact, though it is not pleasant to recall it, that I have on many occasions asserted that in repression the instinctual representative is distorted, displaced, and so on, while the libido belonging to the instinctual impulse is transformed into anxiety. But now an examination of phobias, which should be best able to provide confirmatory evidence, fails to bear out my assertion; it seems, rather, to contradict it directly. The anxiety felt in animal phobias is the ego's fear of castration; while the anxiety felt in agoraphobia (a subject that has been less thoroughly studied) seems to be its fear of sexual temptation—a fear which, after all, must be connected in its origins with the fear of castration. As far as can be seen at present, the majority of phobias go back to an anxiety of this kind felt by the ego in regard to the demands of the libido. It is always the ego's attitude of anxiety which is the primary thing and which sets repression going. Anxiety never arises from repressed libido. If I had contented myself earlier with saying that after the occurrence of repression a certain amount of anxiety appeared in place of the manifestation of libido that was to be expected, I should have nothing to retract today. The description would be correct; and there does undoubtedly exist a correspondence of the kind asserted between the strength of the impulse that has to be repressed and the intensity of the resultant anxiety. But I must admit that I thought I was giving more than a mere description. I believed I had put my finger on a metapsychological process of direct transformation of libido into anxiety. I can now no longer maintain this view. And, indeed, I found it impossible at the time to explain how a transformation of that kind was carried out.'[1]

In discussing exhibitionism Freud wrote: 'The compulsion to exhibit, for instance, is also closely dependent on the castration complex: it is a means of constantly insisting upon the integrity of the subject's own (male) genitals and it reiterates his infantile satisfaction at the absence of a penis in those of women'.[2]

Referring to a type of fetishism Freud stated that 'the foot represents a woman's penis, the absence of which is deeply felt'.[3]

Development of the castration complex in the girl
'*Whereas in boys the Oedipus complex is destroyed by the castration complex, in girls it is made possible and led up to by the castration complex.*'[4]

It should be noted that in these quotations, some of which belong to a late period of Freud's writings, he speaks of the Oedipus complex of the girl as if it were just the opposite of that of the boy, an idea he had given up earlier. This is of importance in that accordingly the attachment to the mother at this phase is therefore viewed as being of a pre-Oedipal nature even though at the same

[1] (1926d) *Inhibitions, Symptoms and Anxiety*, S.E., Vol. 20, p. 108 f.
[2] (1905d) *Three Essays on the Theory of Sexuality*, S.E., Vol. 7, p. 157 n.
[3] [1910] (1905d) ibid., Vol. 7, p. 154 n.
[4] (1925j) 'Some Psychological Consequences of the Anatomical Distinction between the Sexes', S.E.. Vol. 19, p. 256, cf. (1933a) *New Introductory Lectures on Psycho-Analysis*, S.E., Vol. 22, p. 129 f.

time Freud refers to the fact that the little girl has come into the phallic-oedipal phase in which she is a 'masculine being', a 'little man'. In this sense he omits to refer to the first phase of the girl's Oedipus complex as one when her object is the mother, just as she is the object of the boy.

In reference to the scarcity of understanding and information about this phase of the girl's oedipal attachment to the mother Freud points to work done by other authors.

'Abraham's (1921) description of the manifestations of the castration complex in the female is still unsurpassed; but one would be glad if it had included the factor of the girl's original exclusive attachment to her mother. I am in agreement with the principal points in Jeanne Lampl—de Groot's (1927) important paper. In this the complete identity of the pre-Oedipus phase in boys and girls is recognized, and the girl's sexual (phallic) activity towards her mother is affirmed and substantiated by observations. The turning-away from the mother is traced to the influence of the girl's recognition of castration, which obliges her to give up her sexual object, and often masturbation along with it The whole development is summed up in the formula that the girl goes through a phase of the 'negative' Oedipus complex before she can enter the positive one. A point on which I find the writer's account inadequate is that it represents the turning-away from the mother as being merely a change of object and does not discuss the fact that it is accompanied by the plainest manifestation of hostility. To this hostility full justice is done in Helene Deutsch's latest paper, on feminine masochism and its relation to frigidity (1930), in which she also recognizes the girl's phallic activity and the intensity of her attachment to her mother. Helene Deutsch states further that the girl's turning towards her father takes place *via* her passive trends . . .'[1]

Freud describes the girl's entrance into the phallic phase in which she becomes aware of phallic (clitoridal) excitations and of her inferiority in respect to this masculine organ and thus enters the castration complex. 'She makes her judgement and her decision in a flash. She has seen it and knows that she is without it and wants to have it.'[2]

[1] (1931b) 'Female Sexuality', S.E., Vol. 21, p. 241.
[2] (1925j) 'Some Psychological Consequences of the Anatomical Distinction between the Sexes', S.E., Vol. 19, p. 256.

Freud wrote that 'little girls do not resort to denial of this kind [as boys do] when they see that boy's genitals are formed differently from their own. They are ready to recognize them immediately and are overcome by envy for the penis—an envy culminating in the wish, which is so important in its consequences, to be boys themselves'.[1]

'We have learnt from the analysis of many neurotic women that they go through an early age in which they envy their brothers their sign of masculinity and feel at a disadvantage and humiliated because of the lack of it (actually because of its diminished size) in themselves. We include this "envy for the penis" in the "castration complex".[2]

Elsewhere Freud stated it as follows: ' "Anatomy is Destiny" to vary a saying of Napoleon's. The little girl's clitoris behaves just like a penis to begin with; but, when she makes a comparison with a playfellow of the other sex, she perceives that she has "come off badly" [footnote, literally "come off too short"] and she feels this as a wrong done to her and as a ground for inferiority.... A female child, however, does not understand her lack of a penis as being a sex character; she explains it by assuming that at some earlier date she had possessed an equally large organ and then lost it by castration.... The essential difference thus comes about that the girl accepts castration as an accomplished fact, whereas the boy fears the possibility of its occurrence.'[3]

Here what has been named the masculinity complex of women branches off. The wish to become a boy will persist for an indefinite period of time. The second process which may set in Freud calls a 'disavowal', is rather similar to that of the boy before he is in the castration complex. 'Thus a girl may refuse to accept the fact of being castrated, may harden herself in the conviction that she *does* possess a penis, and may subsequently be compelled to behave as though she were a man ... she begins to share the contempt felt by men for a sex which is the lesser in so important a respect, and, at least in holding that opinion, insists on being like a man.',[4]

In the next step, 'Even after penis envy has abandoned its true

[1] [1915] (1905d) *Three Essays on the Theory of Sexuality*, S.E., Vol. 7, p. 195'
[2] (1918a) 'The Taboo of Virginity', S.E., Vol. 11, p. 204.
[3] (1924d) 'The Dissolution of the Oedipus Complex', S.E., Vol. 19, p. 178.
[4] ibid., p. 252 f.

object, it continues to exist: by an easy displacement it persists in the character-trait of *jealousy*. Of course, jealousy is not limited to one sex and has a wider foundation than this, but I am of the opinion that it plays a far larger part in the mental life of women than of men and that is because it is enormously reinforced from the direction of displaced penis envy'. In this context Freud refers to the fantasy 'a child is being beaten' suggesting that the 'child which is being beaten (or caressed) may ultimately be nothing more or less that the clitoris itself, so that at its very lowest level the statement will contain a confession of masturbation, which has remained attached to the content of the formula from its beginning in the phallic phase till later life.

'A third consequence of penis envy seems to be a loosening of the girl's relation to her mother as a love-object. The situation as a whole is not very clear, but it can be seen that in the end the girl's mother, who sent her into the world so insufficiently equipped, is almost always held responsible for her lack of a penis . . .

'There is yet another surprising effect of penis-envy, or of the discovery of the inferiority of the clitoris, which is undoubtedly the most important of all. In the past I had often formed an impression that in general women tolerate masturbation worse than men, that they more frequently fight against it and that they are unable to make use of it in circumstances in which a man would seize upon it as a way of escape without any hesitation. . . . [Freud considers that the reason for this] cannot be anything else than her narcissistic sense of humiliation which is bound up with penis envy, the reminder that after all this is a point on which she cannot compete with boys and that it would therefore be best for her to give up the idea of doing so. Thus the little girl's recognition of the anatomical distinction between the sexes forces her away from masculinity and masculine masturbation on to new lines which lead to the development of femininity.

'So far there has been no question of the Oedipus complex, nor has it up to this point played any part. But now the girl's libido slips into a new position along the line—there is no other way of putting it—of the equation "penis-child". She gives up her wish for a penis and puts in place of it a wish for a child: and *with that purpose in view* she takes her father as a love object. Her mother becomes the object of her jealousy. The girl has turned into a little woman. . . . In girls the Oedipus complex is a secondary formation. The operations of the castration complex precede it and prepare for it ... the castration complex ... inhibits and limits masculinity and encourages femininity.'[1]

Elsewhere Freud commented on the difference in superego formation in the little girl. He wrote that 'The fear of castration being thus excluded in the little girl, a powerful motive also drops out for the setting-up of a superego and for the breaking-off of the infantile genital organization. In her, far more than in the boy, these changes seem to be the result of upbringing and of intimidation from outside which threatens her with a loss of love. The girl's Oedipus complex is much simpler than that of the small bearer of the penis; in my experience, it seldom goes beyond the taking of her mother's place and the adopting of a feminine attitude towards her father. . . .'[2]

He also wrote that ' . . . It does little harm to a woman if she remains in her feminine Oedipus attitude. . . . She will in that case choose her husband for his paternal characteristics and be ready to recognize his authority. Her longing to possess a penis, which is in fact unappeasable, may be satisfied if she can succeed in completing her love for the organ by extending it to the bearer of the organ, just as earlier she progressed from her mother's breast to her mother as whole person.'[3]

Elsewhere Freud stated: 'We can say what the ultimate outcome of the infantile wish for a penis is in women in whom the determinants of a neurosis in later life are absent: it changes into the wish for a *man*, and thus puts up with the man as an appendage to the penis. This transformation, therefore, turns an impulse which is hostile to the female sexual function into one which is favourable to it. Such women are in this way made capable of an erotic life based on the masculine type of object-love, which can exist alongside the feminine one proper, derived from narcissism. We already know that in other cases it is only a baby that makes the transition from narcissistic self-love to object-love possible. So that in this respect too a baby can be represented by the penis.'[4]

Freud occasionally gave examples of the masculinity complex

[1] ibid., p. 254 f.
[2] (1924d) 'The Dissolution of the Oedipus Complex', S.E., Vol. 19, p. 178.
[3] (1940a[1938]) *An Outline of Psycho-Analysis*, S.E., Vol. 23, p. 194.
[4] (1917c) 'On Transformations of Instinct as Exemplified in Anal Erotism', S.E., Vol. 17, p. 129.

in women. He described a type of female frigidity in which a woman will after sexual intercourse give 'unconcealed expression of her hostility towards the man by abusing him, raising her hand against him or actually striking him'.[1]

Later referring to this case, he went on: 'I was able to establish that this phase [of castration complex and penis envy] had existed before that of object-choice. Only later was the little girl's libido directed towards her father, and then instead of wanting to have a penis, she wanted—a child.

'I should not be surprised if in other cases the order in which these impulses occurred were reversed and this part of the castration complex only became effective after a choice of object had been successfully made. But the masculine phase in the girl in which she envies the boy for his penis is in any case developmentally the earlier, and it is closer to the original narcissism than it is to object-love.

'Some time ago I chanced to have an opportunity of obtaining insight into a dream of a newly-married woman which was recognizable as a reaction to the loss of her virginity. It betrayed spontaneously the woman's wish to castrate her young husband and to keep his penis for herself. Certainly there was also room for the more innocent interpretation that what she wished for was the prolongation and repetition of the act, but several details of the dream did not fit into this meaning and the character as well as the subsequent behaviour of the woman who had the dream gave evidence in favour of the more serious view. Behind this envy for the penis, there comes to light the woman's hostile bitterness against the man, which never completely disappears in the relation between the sexes, and which is clearly indicated in the strivings and in the literary productions of "emancipated" women.'[2]

In 'A Case of Homosexuality in a Woman' Freud describes a homosexual female patient who brought along with her from her childhood a strongly marked 'masculinity complex'.

As to the role played by constitutional versus acquired factors with respect to this phenomena complex, Freud wrote:

'A spirited girl, always ready for romping and fighting, she was not at all prepared to be second to her slightly older brother; after

[1] (1918a) 'The Taboo of Virginity', S.E., Vol. 11, p. 201.
[2] ibid., p. 205.

inspecting his genital organs she had developed a pronounced envy for the penis, and the thoughts derived from this envy still continued to fill her mind. She was in fact a feminist; she felt it to be unjust that girls should not enjoy the same freedom as boys, and rebelled against the lot of woman in general. At the time of the analysis the idea of pregnancy and childbirth was disagreeable to her, partly, I surmise, on account of the bodily disfigurement connected with them. Her girlish narcissism had fallen back on this defence, and ceased to express itself as pride in her good looks. Various clues indicated that she must formerly have had strong exhibitionist and scopophilic tendencies. Anyone who is anxious that the claims of acquired as opposed to hereditary factors should not be underestimated in aetiology will call attention to the fact that the girl's behaviour, as described above, was exactly what would follow from the combined effect in a person with a strong mother-fixation of the two influences of her mother's neglect and her comparison of her genital organs with her brother's. It is possible here to attribute to the impress of the operation of external influence in early life something which one would have liked to regard as a constitutional peculiarity. On the other hand, a part even of this acquired disposition (if it *was* really acquired) has to be ascribed to inborn constitution. So we see in practice a continual mingling and blending of what in theory we should try to separate into a pair of opposites—namely, inherited and acquired characters.'[1]

[1] (1920a) 'The Psychogenesis of a Case of Female Homosexuality', S.E., Vol. 18, p. 169.

INDEX

GEORGE ALLEN & UNWIN LTD

Head Office
40 Museum Street, London W.C.1
Telephone: 01-405 8577

Sales, Distribution and Accounts Departments
Park Lane, Hemel Hempstead, Herts.
Telephone: 0442 3244

Athens: 34 Panepistimiou Street
Auckland: P.O. Box 36013, Northcote Central N.4
Barbados: P.O. Box 222, Bridgetown
Beirut: Deeb Building, Jeanne d'Arc Street
Bombay: 103/5 Fort Street, Bombay 1
Buenos Aires: Escritorio 454–459, Florida 165
Calcutta: 285J Bepin Behari Ganguli Street, Calcutta 12
Cape Town: 68 Shortmarket Street
Hong Kong: 105 Wing On Mansion, 26 Hancow Road, Kowloon
Ibadan: P.O. Box 62
Karachi: Karachi Chambers, McLeod Road
Madras: 2/18 Mount Road, Madras
Mexico: Villalongin, 32 Mexico 5, D.F.
Nairobi: P.O. Box 30583
Philippines: P.O. Box 157, Quezon City D-502
Rio de Janeiro: Caixa Postal 2537-Zc-00
Singapore: 36c Prinsep Street, Singapore 7
Sydney N.S.W.: Bradbury House, 55 York Street
Tokyo: C.P.O. Box 1728, Tokyo 100–91
Toronto: 81 Curlew Drive, Don Mills

HAMPSTEAD CLINIC PSYCHOANALYTIC LIBRARY
BASIC PSYCHOANALYTIC CONCEPTS ON THE THEORY OF DREAMS

It is generally accepted that among Freud's many contributions to the understanding of the normal and abnormal aspects of mental functioning, *The Interpretation of Dreams* stands alone and above all others. In this work published in 1900 Freud laid down the foundations of psychoanalytic theory as it was to develop throughout this century. This work not only unravelled the significance of the process of dreaming and allowed for the scientific understanding of the true meaning and nature of the mysterious world of dreams, but created the basis for a general theory of personality capable of encompassing within a single model both the normal and abnormal aspect of mental functioning.

Dr Nagera and his collaborators (all analytically trained) from the Hampstead Child Therapy Clinic and Course (Director, Anna Freud) have isolated from Freud's work twenty-five basic concepts that they consider not only the corner stones of Freud's theory of dreams but fundamental pillars for the understanding of psychoanalytic theory generally. They include subjects such as dream sources, dream work, dream censorship, manifest content, latent content, condensation, displacement, symbolism, secondary revision and dream interpretation. They are presented in a condensed and concentrated manner containing all significant statements made by Freud at any point in his life on the subject of dreams, as well as tracing the historical development of his ideas wherever significant. References to the sources are given in all instances for the guidance of the student of psychoanalysis, the psychiatrist, the social worker, the psychologist or the scholarly minded reader.

LONDON: GEORGE ALLEN AND UNWIN LTD